FROM SURVIVAL TO SAFETY

FROM SURVIVAL TO SAFETY

MY STORY OF ADOPTION AND
INTENTIONAL GROWTH

ANNMARIE SANTAMARINA

NEW DEGREE PRESS

COPYRIGHT © 2023 ANNMARIE SANTAMARINA
All rights reserved.

FROM SURVIVAL TO SAFETY
My Story of Adoption and Intentional Growth

ISBN 979-8-88926-920-5 *Paperback*
      979-8-88926-962-5 *Ebook*

*It was always my intention to dedicate this book to my mom,
Eileen. She taught me so much about maneuvering life's
complexities, especially about getting back up when you fall.
She lived for her children and worried about our safety.
On my birthday, February 27, I sent her this text, "Hi Mom, I want
to thank you for all that you've done for me. You always wanted
us to feel safe. I'm grateful you fought to be my mom. I love you."
That turned out to be the last thing I said to her as she passed
away either that evening or early the next day. Her death came
as a shock to me, and we are enveloped by grief and sadness.
But I also have a deep sense of gratitude that I was able to share
my story with her and let her know what she meant to me.
Mom, you will be missed dearly, and I am sorry you
won't see the final book, but you've always reminded
me to be strong and keep moving forward. I will make
you proud and do just that. May you rest in peace.
Dedicated to Eileen (Shea) Golubinski,
December 3, 1941–February 28, 2023*

CONTENTS

	INTRODUCTION	11
CHAPTER 1.	CHANGE CAN OCCUR WITHOUT CRISIS	17
CHAPTER 2.	ABANDONMENT	35
CHAPTER 3.	ADOPTED BIRDS OF A FEATHER	57
CHAPTER 4.	THE DNA DANCE	71
CHAPTER 5.	BIOLOGICAL LINKS	87
CHAPTER 6.	NOT ALL STORIES HAVE HAPPY ENDINGS	101
CHAPTER 7.	WHY NOW?	113
CHAPTER 8.	MY THREE DADS	127
CHAPTER 9.	HOW OTHERS SEE US VERSUS HOW WE SEE OURSELVES	139
CHAPTER 10.	CAN I OWN MY TRUTH WITHOUT HURTING OTHERS?	155
CHAPTER 11.	AWARENESS AND INTENTION CREATE SELF-CONNECTION	167
CHAPTER 12.	LET GO OF SHAME, KNOW WHEN TO SURRENDER	181
CHAPTER 13.	NEW DATA. NEW STORY.	187
CHAPTER 14.	SAFE AT LAST	197
	ACKNOWLEDGMENTS	203
	APPENDIX	207

When you get to a place where you understand that love and belonging, your worthiness, is a birthright and not something you have to earn, anything is possible.

—BRENÉ BROWN

INTRODUCTION

In January 1992, I moved from New York City to St. Augustine, Florida. I was a month shy of my twenty-fifth birthday, and I just had my whole world blown apart by some news I was not prepared to hear. Turns out I was adopted as a baby, but my mother never found the right time to tell me until that moment. I have struggled with abandonment issues my entire life. I did not understand until recently these were intertwined with my adoption, even though I had spent the first twenty-five years of my life without knowing I was adopted.

My family moved to St. Augustine five years earlier, and I had stayed behind in New York, nineteen years old at the time, to work and attend college. Balancing the responsibilities of my studies and a job became too much, so I moved to Florida to focus on my degree. Within a week of my arrival, my mother shared with me that she was really happy I had moved, and she needed to tell me some things.

I can be slightly sarcastic, especially as a defense mechanism, so I was kidding when I retorted, "Oh really? Like what? That I am adopted?"

At that moment, the color drained from her face, and she replied, "Actually yes, that's exactly what I wanted to talk about with you. I adopted you as a baby and have not told you because I could never find the right time."

With this news came many questions and some realizations that would take years for me to truly understand. One thing was for certain: I would never be the same. My entire existence was disrupted in that one moment.

The disruption wasn't because being adopted was a bad thing but due to the shock that all I believed to be true was a lie. I was betrayed by my family, and my identify was totally blown up.

Over the following thirty years, I thought about finding my biological family. I had made some early attempts to get more information about my birth parents but kept hitting dead ends. Once I encountered a roadblock, I seemed to always find an excuse to avoid pursuing my search further.

Then I took a course called The Rewrite, where the objective was to identify a story we tell ourselves and rewrite it with new data. I chose "When people get to know me, they leave." This was my story of abandonment and not fully belonging anywhere. I carried this around with all sorts of compiled evidence, like one would carry around a backpack filled with diaries of days past and outdated notions. Through this work

I realized my feelings of abandonment could be traced back to my birth when my biological parents decided to give me up. I had created limiting beliefs, such as "I am not worthy" and "Why would people choose me?" Then I developed patterns that anchored me to this self-critical narrative.

Over the past ten years, I made a pivot in my life and started to face and address some of my fears. I worked with coaches and healers and embarked on a journey to better understand and give myself permission to be who I truly am. Until that point, I had put a lot of emphasis on who others expected me to be, hoping they would like me and not leave.

That work led me here, back to adoption and the role it has played in my life. Also, I finally allowed myself to admit out loud that I believe we all have a purpose, and everything happens for a reason. We are being guided, and if we allow ourselves to be open, magic can happen. I felt the time was now, and I became determined to understand the roots of my origin and the circumstances that led to my birth and adoption. The deeper I dove into the facts around my adoption, my curiosity widened beyond my own story.

I have friends who are adopted or have adopted children themselves. They have generously shared their experiences with me. The more I talk with others, I am discovering how many people are affected not only by adoption but also by all sorts of family estrangement and have created their own internal dialogues, which impact their lives.

In researching some of the data around adoption, I learned in 1967—the year I was born—158,000 adoptions took place, which calculated to 44.9 adoptions per 1,000 live births that year (Johnston 2022).

Being connected to adoption is not uncommon for American families. According to Adoption Network statistics, one out of every twenty-five families with children have adopted, and about 115,343 children are adopted each year (Adoption Network 2023).

The data led me to consider the relationship between our origin story and the stories we create in our lives. I prioritized the search for my biological family and successfully identified and located both maternal and paternal relatives. I experienced disappointment and repeated rejections, a blatant denial of my existence. Conversely, I encountered other family members who openly received and embraced my presence. I have learned with adoption, and family estrangement in general, shame, guilt, secrets, denial, betrayal, and confusion often occur. People will react according to where they are in their lives, and sometimes their reaction has very little to do with us. Their reaction certainly does not define us.

Through this journey, I have been able to extricate negativity and limiting beliefs I imposed on myself, which were mostly based on my interpretation of others' actions. I have encountered a new level of freedom and sense of self.

For most of my life I gave away my personal power because of the meaning I attached to events over which I had no control. I am recalibrating that original data rooted in stories of abandonment and not belonging, especially the core belief "If someone gets to know me, they will leave."

I have found new data to support stories that are more in alignment with who I am. I found value in myself without validation from others. I recognized my codependent behaviors and the struggles they were creating in my relationships and life. The more I grow, the more growth I crave.

For my readers, this book may be of interest to you if you believe our interactions with others define and shape our own beliefs about ourselves and the meaning we attach to them. If you have experienced any sort of rejection or abandonment and believed it was because of something you did or said, you find will value in the pages ahead.

I have shared anecdotes from my own life, which hopefully you will find relatable. Perhaps you have given away your power in some capacity, or you've gotten caught up in blaming others for your circumstances and possibly feel you are a victim.

If you understand mindset can affect outcomes and behaviors and you believe there is always an opportunity to turn a negative situation or reaction into a lesson that can be valuable for your own growth, you will enjoy this book. If you are open to the understanding that we don't always have control over what happens, but we *do* always have control over how we react to what happens, the personal entries I share in this book may resonate with you.

If you are on any sort of personal growth path and need a push forward, or do not know where to start, then begin with my journey. May it inspire you to grow yourself and the stories shaping or affecting your life. My intention is to be transparent and vulnerable with you. Some of the things I share are hard to see on paper, yet I believe they are critical to owning my truth and sharing my experiences.

If you have just one takeaway, may it be recognition that you are not alone. You might feel stuck and want to make new choices but have been putting them off or allowing fear to hold you back. It is my wish that this book will help you not hold back any longer.

CHAPTER 1

CHANGE CAN OCCUR WITHOUT CRISIS

IT STARTED IN MY CHILDHOOD
My childhood was riddled with chaos and disruption and bordered on crisis almost daily. I didn't know life could be easy and things could fall into place. I spent many years sabotaging anything good that happened to protect myself and stay ahead of the ultimate decimation I believed was waiting for me. The defense mechanisms I built ruined many promising opportunities, but I always "landed on my feet," so I understood this was how I was supposed to live.

You may hear these as harsh sentiments. I find myself censoring them in my mind as I write. The truth can hurt, and this is the truth.

I was forty-plus years old when I realized change did not need to be precipitated by crisis. You don't have to react to make a change. You certainly don't need to blow things up because you want something different. You can simply decide and opt to make necessary modifications at any given time.

A whole new way of thinking and being awakened for me.

A deeper understanding of the relationship between survival and safety emerged as well. The notion that I had spent my life existing in survival mode crystalized. I had never felt safe and was always anticipating the next bad thing.

Thankfully, I discovered I could make other choices. All was not lost. Through work with incredible teachers, guides, and the acquisition of valuable tools, I adjusted my perspective and the concept of safety shifted for me. I am safe.

You might ask, "Well, what does that mean exactly?"

We tend to follow patterns we are taught, which in my case makes sense. My mother grew up in survival mode, and she transferred these learned behaviors to her own life. Her mother lived in a constant state of chaos, and she repeated that cycle. When my mom was growing up, my grandmother was single more than with a partner and they moved often, usually under drastic measures. My mother did not have the opportunity to learn or experience what a stable lifestyle or environment was.

It was not as extreme with us. We always had a place, though it was never the same for long. We moved frequently during my childhood, similar to my grandmother and her kids. From kindergarten to sixth grade, I attended a different school each year.

Changing schools and neighborhoods as a young child was not ideal. For my youngest grades, I can't recall any specific memory about where we lived nor the actual transitions. My first distinct memory was from the second grade. I had a teacher, Mrs. Ammirati, who made me feel seen and included.

When I learned at the end of that year I would not be returning in the fall, I felt sad to leave my friends and feared the unknown. It was the first time I actively prepared for the worst. The critical thoughts inevitably came to mind. *Would I be accepted by the kids in my new class? Would I be able to make any friends? How long before we had to leave again?*

I was always the new kid. I had to adjust quickly and make new friends repeatedly. Some years, I didn't know I wouldn't be back in September. This left unfinished business, and friendships fell away due to circumstances.

By the fourth and fifth grade, I stopped getting attached. I assumed I wouldn't be there long, knowing we would ultimately move. I later realized the protective measures I had built at that age stayed with me long into adulthood. I searched for evidence my partner or friends would eventually leave. I especially struggled with groups of friends and the deep fear I would be left out or dumped.

No one talked about trauma and the impact traumatic events leave on a person, not even the therapists I worked with. The effects of these early experiences and the scars they left took decades to fully understand and ultimately heal.

When I was eight years old, my mother married her third husband, John. He was the person who taught me stability and safety. He represented a significant turning point in my life. Of course, I was eight and didn't comprehend the value he brought until much later.

Once they married things became slightly more settled, though we still moved each year until I was in the seventh grade. Finally, we were in the same place for four years, only to move when I started high school. I was utterly devastated. It placed me into a different zone, affecting where I would go. I thought I had to start all over again. John knew how upset I was, and he offered an alternate outcome. He drove me every day to the bus, so I could attend Franklin K. Lane high school, where I was supposed to go.

John recognized my craving for consistency, though I am not sure he nor I understood the abandonment part then.

I used to think something was wrong with me because I always felt unsettled. A phrase I've used often is "Waiting for the other shoe to drop." Even when things were going well, the thought that permeated my brain was, *Don't get too comfortable; things will shake up eventually.*

I had no evidence that showed me life could be easy and in flow. When things were good, I typically thought something bad was lurking around the corner, waiting to pounce and throw my life into a state of disarray.

During my senior year of high school, the biggest shoe so far fell. We learned John's job was closing their Brooklyn plant, and our family had to move to Kansas or Florida (St. Augustine). I did not want to move! I was set to go to Baruch College in Manhattan. I originally wanted to go away, but my mother forbode that as an option. As a result, a series of events and decisions unfolded, which reinforced my feelings about not belonging and would play into my story in a larger way as the years went on.

Ironically, this was not the biggest disruption of my life. I had not yet learned I was adopted.

COACHING PROVIDED A NEW PERSPECTIVE ON OLD BELIEFS

When something upsetting occurs, consider it an opportunity to see what's provoking the need to react.

One of my coaches, Lara, says, "Access is in the upset."

By zooming out and taking space, you might be able to extract a lesson. Through focused introspection, you pinpoint a situation or a person that is not in alignment with your highest self. The challenge is to invite insight and awareness, especially when you find yourself in uncomfortable situations.

The term highest self may not be familiar to everyone. Think of it as the part of you that is unencumbered by ego. Other words that might be used when referring to higher self are soul or spirit. From the simplest point, your higher self is the version of you that rises above the elements when things get tough. Your higher self comes from a healed place not a wounded one. When your higher self is in charge, you can dissect a problem from a centered position through a mindset of gratitude, love, and abundance.

"Access is in the upset" is something I've come to rely on within my toolkit. It took time to remove the layers of armor I had developed before I was open to the concept. My stories and old beliefs kept me stuck in a place where I didn't believe a new perspective was plausible. As I unraveled them little by little and reframed my thoughts about why things happened, I noticed I was less reactive. Bad things happen. That's life. How I handled them shifted tremendously.

This was a stark transition from the generational chaos and crisis pattern I had known since childhood. I found it refreshing those rational explanations existed when things went awry. I released the idea that I was being punished. A whole new light was shed on how to resolve conflict. Some people use the expression "Everything happens for a reason." It is similar, but I like Lara's approach because it encourages you to dig deeper and not just shrug it off as if we had no other choice.

This is a good time to address the concepts I present, which may be unfamiliar or potentially cause you discomfort, such as the higher self explanation offered earlier. If you are not a spiritual or religious person and experience resistance to any terms outlined in the book, I encourage you to just go with it. Regardless of your belief system, whether it comes to God, the Universe, or Source, ideally we can all agree not everything is within our control.

I reference ideas that span all sorts of backgrounds and will do my best to provide you with as much supporting information as possible. These ideas can be as simple as how to gain a better understanding of your values and how you apply them in your life. My request is you remain open and receptive to having your best experience while reading this book and applying some of the principles, should you choose to.

PATTERNS ARE DEEPLY EMBEDDED IN OUR THOUGHTS AND ACTIONS
When you live in a certain pattern, it can be difficult to see an alternate point of view or recognize another outcome is possible. Especially when we've known a certain way our entire life. Owning the role we play in perpetuating behaviors and patterns can be hard. I am not suggesting we are responsible for all the things that happen to us, but I do believe we play an active part in how we live as well as what and who we attract.

Changing my patterns started ten years ago when I worked with my first coach. I had seen a few therapists in my twenties and thirties, seeking to alter certain behaviors, but wasn't successful. None of these therapists brought forth the role my thoughts and beliefs played in my behavior, which, looking back, feels odd. I built a reputation of being confrontational, controlling, and angry. I had a quick tongue and lashed out when I was feeling cornered or let down.

My natural instincts are to verbalize my feelings, but I was taught to repress and deny them. My self-expression was discouraged. Asking for what I wanted was considered selfish behavior and wasn't tolerated and was typically berated.

When I mustered the courage to ask, and my needs were not met, I didn't know how to manage my disappointment. Since I was denied the opportunity to think or speak for myself, I had very little experience communicating my feelings, good or bad. My mom often contradicted me and provided her own evaluation of what I was feeling versus what I felt. Her interpretations were usually disconnected from my reality.

I carried the labels of "angry" and "confrontational" imposed on me by my mother, boyfriends, bosses, and some friends through various altercations. I took ownership of the version of me that was created on my behalf. I started to believe what was said about me. I did not have my own identity. Nor did I have the capacity to protect my true self, especially since I had no idea who that was. I became buried under everyone else's opinions of me.

If I were to evaluate those times and incidents through the lens of "Access is in the upset," I would say what typically triggered my angry and aggressive behavior was feeling left out, betrayed, or abandoned. In a situation where I was treated poorly and I felt I was not good enough, I retreated to my default defense. My instincts were to fight back. I had learned to survive.

When I was young, my mom called me "pissy eyes." I was prone to tears as an instinctual expression, and it made her uncomfortable. She thought if she called me a name, I would toughen and cry less. Her insults turned out to be counterintuitive to the development of my confidence and ability to express myself. Her goal was to make me stronger. Instead, she forced me to stifle my emotions, which resulted in continued denial of self.

I coped by bottling up my emotions. What I didn't realize was how badly I spoke to myself. *You have no right to be upset*, or *No one is going to care if you say anything anyway. Be a grown-up and don't complain to others about your feelings.*

The downside to this approach? I was completely out of alignment. I wanted to express myself freely but did not have a safe place to.

At some point, everything I had been holding inside erupted and flowed out like lava pouring from a volcano. This reinforced my reputation as an angry and aggressive bitch.

MY RELATIONSHIPS SUFFERED
With friends, my behavior was exacerbated by alcohol. With boyfriends, my behavior was triggered by insecurity. My needs were not met. I did not have the tools or words to ask. I kept quiet, but inside I was bursting with unresolved emotion, and this usually ended badly.

Typically, I said something nasty or stormed out of a place, which provoked tension. The people involved felt awkward and usually blindsided. Nothing got resolved, and I felt crappy about myself and my reactions.

In one relationship I got physical. I was so frustrated, I punched him. Once I physically broke things. These were not my finest moments, and I am not proud of them.

I didn't think I was worthy to ask of others. When I finally worked up the courage to ask for my needs to be met, I was let down or dismissed. I displayed anger. My feelings encompassed varied emotions, including but not always limited to: disappointment, sadness, unworthiness, betrayal, loneliness, unimportance, and a general disconnect. I was never taught to decipher emotions, so they all got lumped into one broad category—anger. I wore my anger like a badge.

When I finally connected my upsets to access, I was able to decode those emotions on a deeper level. My capacity in certain situations expanded. I started to look back on incidents that had occurred throughout my life from a completely new vantage point.

One of my early relationships dug deep into the well of my worst fears and insecurities. I was dating this guy for six months when I was contacted by a woman who told me he had a girlfriend. Turned out he had been lying to me and was still in a relationship with his ex. He told me they had broken up. This played directly into my abandonment stories.

I had the courage to break up with him, but he came back a few months later and swore to me his relationship with her was finally over. I honestly can't recall if I believed or trusted him, but we reconciled. We moved in together, even though I was insecure, jealous, and unsure. I didn't know how to articulate my fears. Nor did I have the confidence to stand up for myself. Even if I did, would he even care? When I finally shared my emotions, they were raw, unfiltered, and looked mostly like anger and jealousy. He was dismissive and said my behavior was the problem, not his.

Yet again, I was labeled as needy and clingy. I held on tightly, which made us fight more. A woman coworker entered the picture, and I sensed something. He told me I was nuts and highlighted my jealousy and insecurity. He ended up cheating on me with her and turned it around to blame me.

A part of me accepted responsibility for his infidelity. *If I was not so jealous, needy, angry, and confrontational, I would have been enough, and he would not have felt the need to cheat on me.* I rationalized my behavior was commensurate with his infidelity. His reaction to blame me was gaslighting.

Reflecting on that time through my healed heart, I understand my insecurities were related to my own feelings of unworthiness. I recognize my jealousy was due to his original betrayal. He lost my trust and never put any energy into trying to regain it. My anger was directed by hurt and believing I was not enough. I had proof from prior experiences, which suggested anyone I loved would leave. I didn't have a strong foundation to trust he could be wholly satisfied in a relationship with me or he would choose me.

We all have experienced broken hearts. I opted to share this story because it demonstrates my active participation that easily portrays me as a victim. The flipped script on that version is I had choices. However, I didn't recognize that to be the case. I didn't believe I was worthy of anything better, so I accepted his behavior and his definition of me. I allowed this person to have more power in my life than he deserved. The irony of this tale is he refuses to speak to me, as if he were the wronged party.

I've let go of any resentment toward him, and I see I had an opportunity to learn and grow from this relationship. I suppose he was fighting his own demons. He couldn't leave any relationship because he was unhappy. Instead, he cheated and created crisis to force a change.

AWARENESS OF MY EMOTIONS HELPED ME SEE THINGS DIFFERENTLY

A friend who is a psychologist introduced me to the concept of primary and secondary emotions. He explained primary emotions are natural, instinctive experiences that are typically good. Secondary emotions are more of a learned response to cover up complex emotions with a less sensitive emotion. Anger is the most common secondary emotion. We have been generally conditioned that it's not okay to be sad or vulnerable, so anger becomes a convenient replacement to cover up those less acceptable feelings. What looks like anger on the surface is often a protective cover for feelings like fear, hurt, worry, or sadness. Disappointment and lack of acceptance were two emotions I personally put an anger protective cover on.

The imposition of my adoptive mother and her inability to process her own emotions crippled me. She was not comfortable standing up for herself, and I suspect when I tried to, rather than support me, she opted to shut me down.

Her usual feedback was, "Don't make this a big deal, AnnMarie. You are overreacting."

I lived my life buying into other people's opinions of me, which led to me believing false beliefs about who I am. I refer to this as giving away your power.

This has become an incredibly empowering notion for me. I am not suggesting we don't take responsibility for our behavior. Nor do I believe we can blame others for our negative emotions and reactions.

Facing our emotions head-on is powerful. I am still doing the work, and sometimes I want to resist or avoid it. But I know when I allow myself the gift of exploration to understand why I am reacting the way I am, awareness and insights abound. If I sit in blame, I am responsible for perpetuating the pattern.

Another lesson I learned from Lara, "When you blame others, you give away your power."

Worthiness was not taught in my household. My mom used this phrase a lot, "Oh, you think you are too big for your britches." As a child I was frequently told I was selfish. When you are told things enough, you believe them. I don't know what my mom saw in me that caused her to tell me these things. I don't know what she believed to be true either. I started acting in ways to make her comfortable, even if they didn't feel right to me.

In my mid-thirties I realized I was keeping myself small and holding back any good things that were happening to make my mom comfortable. I sought out crisis in my life and emphasized it so I could talk to her. I believed she needed my siblings and I to need her. I thought I had to be these things to get her love. We were keeping codependency alive.

I see now I never gave her a chance to do things differently. Not only did I not try to break the pattern with her, but I also attracted other people into my life who kept the energy of this codependent nature at the forefront.

MY DISCOVERIES WITH ENERGY WORK
When I started working with Lara, I unfolded a brand-new way of thinking. She is an energy coach. At first it seemed very abstract. I had trouble conceiving how it all worked. I was curious and I liked Lara, so I went with it. She was wonderfully down-to-earth and had astute business sense. She still does.

I paid special attention to how I felt working with her. During and shortly after our sessions, I physically felt shifts in my body. If I did the homework assignments, I had results in between sessions. I knew this approach was working, and I was changing, little by little.

I was holding on to negative energy and deeply repressed emotions, which resulted in physical ailments. My left leg went numb frequently, and my shoulders were always locked and super tight. I went for massages and experienced temporary relief, but the tension in my body quickly returned.

We worked to push the stagnant energy out, and I noticed longer-term effects and results, mentally, physically, and energetically. Sometimes during our sessions I experienced movement and pulses throughout my body.

I shared, "Wow, I just felt that move through my left leg. My chest was tight but now it feels open."

After a session I felt lighter and more agile. We tested my body to determine where the stuck energy lay dormant. Once we narrowed the location, we focused on identifying what emotion or old story was attached to the stagnant energy. Lara provided me with a phrase that affirmed a reframe on the belief I was holding on to.

One belief that often came up for me was the "fear of not belonging," and the affirmation Lara provided me to reframe was "I am one with all that is."

"All that is" meaning the Universe, being guided and protected by the divine, and God. This affirmation reassured me I was not alone. I had available help and resources—if I was willing to receive.

When the stagnant energy cleared, yawning followed. Lara explained the yawns represented the energy clearing, as with most deep breaths. This was the beginning of an awakening. I discovered newfound awareness, and energy work turned out to be the beginning of many tools to guide me as I maneuvered uncharted waters ahead.

The work is ongoing, and these types of changes take time. With forty-five years living a certain way, I couldn't expect energy work once a week to be enough. I continued to expand. I took courses, practiced meditation, and learned about chakras (more energy centers). I tried Reiki as a recipient and then became Reiki Level 1 certified.

The key to all this? I broadened my perspective. I said yes, even if I didn't fully understand or was afraid. I am still saying yes.

I have a new outlook. You create change for a myriad of reasons. Whether it is the right timing, you have a deep yearning for a change, or you are ready to leave behind something that no longer serves you, change does not have to be in reaction to anything, especially not crisis.

CHANGE REALLY WAS POSSIBLE
When my business partner and I ran our tech company for twenty years, we had days when we felt like we were done. We worked in IT and it was stressful, especially in the early days. My old behaviors and patterns showed up in my day-to-day life and in my workplace. I yelled at the staff, I was anxious about finding clients or getting paid, and I was irritated often.

During intense and heated moments, one of us would say, "Maybe it's time to sell."

Each time that happened, I responded, "I don't want to decide to sell in reaction to something. I want to sell because we are moving toward a greater goal, the next best step."

Even though my triggers still existed, I was better at noticing I didn't want to create outcomes through crisis any longer.

My partner respected this decision. In 2018, we finally found the right firm to acquire us. We brokered a deal that made the most sense for everyone involved. This was a shining moment of empowerment. I had broken a long-standing pattern in my life. We didn't fight. Neither of us stormed off, slammed doors, or erupted into anger or disagreement. We were not in crisis. We were in growth. It felt amazing and powerful, and I wanted to create more experiences like that.

STEPPING INTO MY POWER

I am currently on the edge of more change, including stepping out of my prior role in IT as I continue to evolve.

I see many opportunities on the horizon, and I invite these changes and expansion into my life. I have taken on new roles, such as author and coach, helping others to step into their higher selves. I am cultivating existing roles including wife, daughter, sister, and friend.

I am growing out of roles that no longer serve me. Though it was hard to let go of being an owner and in charge, I recognized I had reached my capacity in that situation. I loved working with my IT clients, but I also felt limited to what I could ultimately deliver.

Now when I work with clients, I provide more expansive and deeper interactions. Technology is one component, but

I focus on varied aspects of their businesses and lives, which feels inspiring and exciting.

I invite more of what I want into my life now. I am prioritizing myself and my needs. No crisis is necessary to create the change I want in my life!

If you've felt confined by the patterns or limiting beliefs that have been created on your behalf, don't despair. It is never too late to take back your power. You can decide and invite your own new beginnings and outcomes, and they do not have to be in reaction to any crisis.

How can you take the lessons I've shared and apply them to your own circumstances? Try identifying one pattern that feels like it's in a loop. What action can you take? Where has there been upset in your life? What can you access about an upset to find a new meaning or a potential lesson?

CHAPTER TWO

ABANDONMENT

I have deep-rooted fears about being left out, left behind, or abandoned. I have told myself a story for almost five and a half decades that says, "When people get to know the real me, they leave."

THE ORIGINAL TRAUMA
Because I am adopted, my feelings of abandonment started in my biological mother's womb. The trauma of adoption was exacerbated since I was not told until I was twenty-five years old. When I learned I had been given up at birth, it felt like the original abandonment. *How could my biological mother give birth to three children before me and decide to keep them but not me?* The only possible explanation had to be I was not good enough.

I tried to consider my biological mother's perspective and wondered what that decision was like for her. *Was it painful for her to decide she could not keep me? Did she think about me often? Or ever? Did my siblings know about me?* I agonized over these unknown details. I thought about this family who went on as if I had never existed, not even missing my presence in their lives.

Sometimes my curiosity ran deeper. *What was her pregnancy like? Did she know she would not raise me from the moment she found out? If not, how did she come to that conclusion? What was it like for her when she was giving birth? Who was my father? Was he involved?*

She had been through this three times already, but this pregnancy was different. This child was not going home and instead was being removed from her life. *Did knowing that affect her during the pregnancy or my birth? Did trauma exist before my life even started?*

I did not truly understand the impact of my abandonment story, nor how much power it had over me.

Varied instances of abandonment are interwoven within the fabric of my life, and some have left greater residue than others. A few are so strongly ingrained into my memory I can easily return to those moments when it felt like I'd been extinguished from someone's life, as if I never existed in the first place.

If something happens to you enough times, you believe it as the only truth. As I developed relationships, my insecurities heightened. A dialogue developed in my mind and consistently played as a background soundtrack. *Will this person even show up?* If they did show up, my next thought was, *How long before they get tired of me and leave?*

These beliefs infiltrated how I spoke to myself. My constant internal critic told me I was not and would never be enough. I was convinced this was the reason why people left me or gave up. I believed I was unworthy of permanent love and inclusion. These are known as limiting beliefs, which are versions of stories about you that you take on as truth. You create behaviors based on your limiting beliefs and your experiences are captured through this filter.

ADOPTION RESEARCH IS SCARCE

Was I the only person who had this problem? I was not familiar with terms like limiting beliefs or ego and higher self until later in life. As I opened myself up to the possibility I was not alone, I looked for evidence of other adoptees having similar thoughts and experiences.

I haven't found much clinical research about the connection between adoption and relationship issues. I discovered articles and anecdotes from other adoptees describing their stories.

One article on the American Adoptions website shares the following philosophy:

Adopted adults and relationships issues are unavoidable, some people say. *Adoptees can't properly bond with anyone in their life due to the trauma they experienced at the hands of their birth mother when placed for adoption.*

Issues involving adoptees and intimate relationships are often assumed to be the result of the original trauma from birth mother separation. Some adoptees and adoption researchers hypothesize that when an infant is separated from the woman they bonded with for the nine months in utero, it affects their future attachment styles (American Adoption 2023).

This article continues that other aspects of adoption may impact current and future relationships for adoptees, such as:

- **Fear of rejection**: which can manifest as the desire to reject a person before they can reject you.
- **Low self-esteem**: which can manifest as not feeling worthy of love or choosing partners who treat you poorly because you don't feel you deserve better.
- **Fear of abandonment**: which can make you feel paranoid about your partner leaving you.
- **Fear of change**: which can make you want to stay in unhealthy relationships or compel you to avoid new relationships or growth within a relationship.

This all resonated with me. Even before the age of twenty-five, I experienced all the above. *Does that suggest I was affected by adoption, even without knowing?*

ADOPTIVE PARENTS PLAYED A SIGNIFICANT ROLE

By way of background, my adoptive mother married her first husband, whom I get the name Santamarina from. I believed he was my biological father, and I still carry his name. I understood they divorced when I was three years old. During the writing of this book, I became aware of new information. They married and divorced twice. I learned they both had a business reason to marry again after their first divorce. My mother's reason was she wanted to adopt a baby.

Allegedly she told him, "I will do this for you, but I want a baby, and they won't give one to a single mother. You will stay until the adoption is finalized."

I don't know if the situation played out exactly this way. This information was presented to me after she passed away, so I cannot confirm with her. When she was still alive, she told me she threatened him not to leave before the adoption process completed.

As I recall, their relationship was emotionally tumultuous. At times I felt I was in the middle, even if it was unintentional, and neither of them realized.

When speaking with my adoptive father's daughter, she told me her parents married in August 1969. I was eighteen months old at that time, so he was likely gone from my life by the time I was one year old.

That explains why I don't remember him from my early childhood. He moved to Arizona, and I remained in New York City with my adoptive mom.

What confused me was my mother forced me to maintain a relationship with him. I've wondered if I was an excuse so she could stay connected to him. He showed no interest in me. As far as I was concerned, he abandoned me.

She often told me, "You need to call your father."

I called and talked to him but felt nothing. This was confusing to me. *How could I not feel anything?* We shared the same DNA. *How could I not have anything in common with him? I must be broken.* That was the only reasonable explanation why I could not relate to my father.

She also told me, "You need to tell him you love him when you hang up the phone."

I stoically replied, "Love him? I don't even know him."

The messages I received were conflicting and imposing, especially between the ages of eight and thirteen. I was told how I was supposed to feel but didn't. I was expected to love this man, yet he was never there physically or emotionally. All I knew was he left when I was a baby. In my version of this story, he got to know me and was like, "Nope. This one is not worth it."

"I am out of here!" is what I envisioned he said when he bolted.

This version reinforced my abandonment story.

The summer before high school, I visited him and his family in Arizona, a decision that was made for me. I was fourteen years old and had never been on a plane. *Was this a sane and rational plan?* I was scared. No one seemed to care. I flew to Syracuse and met up with his wife and their two kids. Together we flew the rest of the way to Arizona so I could spend two weeks with a man who was practically a stranger and his family.

The month before the trip, I had horrible nightmares of my plane crashing, once over the Atlantic Ocean and another time in Switzerland. Clearly, I was not doing too well in geography. In my defense, this was a big trip for a fourteen-year-old whose furthest trip had been to Cape May, New Jersey. I dreamed about it multiple times. It felt so real, I could feel my body tensing up and my stomach dropping as the plane crashed into the water. I had no control over the dreams, much in the same way I had no say about the trip.

THE TRIP FELT LIKE A PUNISHMENT
Perhaps I could have seen the trip as an adventure, but it felt more like a punishment. No one cared how I felt or bothered to consider my angst, even when I told them. The blatant disregard for my feelings, especially when I had the guts to share, anchored my belief that I didn't matter.

His wife was nice, but I felt like a stranger in their lives. She cooked breakfast every morning, and that was the highlight of the day. He went to work early and came home around 2:00 p.m., then he sat in his chair until he nodded off. I waited to spend time with him. I thought the point of the trip was to bond with my father.

I thought my brother and sister (his kids) lived an exciting life and did all sorts of things with our father. This was not my experience at all. Perhaps things were different when the weirdo big sister from New York City was not visiting. It all felt very painful and boring, *maybe that was because of me? Maybe they had fun when I was not there.* They had a pool in the backyard, but it was August in Arizona, so the water was like bathwater! No respite in sight.

I have spoken to his daughter as adults, and she shared that he did the same with them every day when he got home from work.

One day they'd planned a trip to the mall, and mentioned roller skating. Finally, something to look forward to. I carefully chose my outfit, so excited to spend time with my dad! I went downstairs for breakfast, and he wasn't there. I asked for him, and his wife informed us he had to work so he would not be joining. I was completely deflated. He clearly did not have any interest in knowing me. He was the opposite of John, who always interacted with my siblings and me. He always took us places and actively engaged in activities with us.

The trip was cloaked in expectations. My mother expected me to create a relationship with my father. He was not participating, or even trying. My father allegedly wanted me there but did not make any effort to get to know me. I wanted so badly to be seen, for him to care about me. I wanted him to take an interest in me. That never happened. It was exhausting, confusing, and a lot of pressure.

I did not have much in common with his kids. They were younger than me, my half-brother by three years and my half-sister by six. They probably didn't want anything to do with me either.

FOMO

The other factor at play was how badly I missed my friend group back home. It was 1981 and we didn't have texts, social media, or any immediate way to stay in contact. It felt like I was gone for a lifetime. I may have invented FOMO (fear of missing out) because all I could think about was what my friends were doing without me. We wrote letters while I was away. A few days before the trip ended, I received one that read,

"We all had a conversation and have decided we should not be friends in high school. When we start school in September, we will no longer be hanging out. It's been easier without you here, and we think its best if we keep it that way."

They dumped me! More abandonment evidence and reinforcement of my story.

It was a few weeks until I started high school, and I had zero friends. My greatest fear had come true. It turned out to be a blessing but tell that to a tortured fourteen-year-old who is stuck in the desert with her fake father.

My eighth-grade science teacher must have had strong intuition.

She wrote in my graduation book, "Santa, you can't soar like an eagle when you hang with turkeys!"

If I understood the Universe back then, I would have recognized that sentiment as a precursor to a future upset. I was not enlightened then, so I had no way to understand I was being protected. I was a rejected and heartbroken teenager who was not good enough for her father to love and accept her and not cool enough for her friends to miss or value her. My absence presented an opportunity for them to kick me to the curb.

These varied instances seemed to take me to the same dark thought, "When people get to know me, they leave."

FOMO stayed with me and resulted in issues within many of my friendships, especially when groups were involved. A group of three or any odd number was specifically challenging. I got upset when friends made plans that didn't include me. I was paranoid any omission was intentional and hurtful. This was a painful way to live. My behavior was triggered by the events of my childhood and the beliefs I convinced myself were true. I was always on high alert, looking for signs they were trying to get rid of me. If I proved it before the abandonment happened, I would avoid being blindsided again.

GOOD THINGS CAN HAPPEN
As if there was not enough going on for me personally, the air traffic controllers went on strike. My flight home was canceled, and I had to stay in Arizona for another two weeks. I called my mom in hysterics and insisted I could not stay. They were not my family, and I was done.

John was ready to drive to Arizona. Thankfully, we had a better plan. His sister lived in Tucson with her husband! They rescued me and took me to their house until I could get a flight back home. He worked for a newspaper, and we visited his job. I decided I wanted to be a journalist during that encounter. I loved the newsroom atmosphere and thought I would work for a newspaper someday.

We went out to the desert and watched lightning storms. John and I did this together during our family vacations to Cape May. It was our thing. The familiarity made me feel safe. I felt more connected to my stepdad's sister, who had already been my aunt for six years, than I did to my biological father and his family. I didn't know then he was not my biological father.

I don't remember the flight home, nor flying by myself or any part of the return trip. I recall a horrible situation that got better. I was grateful to my aunt and her husband for taking me to Tucson. They helped me create good memories from an otherwise dismal circumstance.

When I returned to New York, it was time to start high school. My resilient nature took the wheel. I was heartbroken by the letdown from my so-called friends. However, I recovered. I made new friends and reconnected with old ones, some of which are still friends today.

My high school experience was overall good with less chaos and disruption than my younger years until I was a senior, when John found out his company was leaving New York. He either relocated the family or lost his job. This was the only job he had ever worked in his adult life.

ABANDONED BY MY OWN FAMILY
They made the decision to move to St. Augustine, Florida. This was a big interruption to my plans.

I had already decided to attend college in New York. Ironically, I wanted to go away when I first started the application process. My mother was adamant I would stay in New York. Once again, a plan was devised based on a certain set of facts. Then crisis/change erupted, and those facts became irrelevant—another theme that continued to persist in my life.

I attended a full year in college before they moved, and then I went to work full time. I had to be financially responsible and able to support myself. I continued to take classes part time, in the early mornings and evenings. My family left New York in December 1986. I stayed and lived with a family friend. My mother, father, younger sister, and brother went to Florida to start a new life.

This felt like abandonment. I was an outsider in my family, and I was on my own. I was nineteen. Of course, I had the choice to go, but that did not feel like much of a choice to me at the time.

As I reflect on that time in my life, a lot of struggles ensued over the next five years. I filed for bankruptcy, grappled with relationship failures, worked full time, and tried to get my college degree. It became too much of a burden. After the most recent breakup, I was ready to throw in the towel.

I called my parents and told them I wanted to come "home" to finish college.

My mother responded, "I don't need your weepy ass here, all depressed on my sofa and in my house. Get your life together and be a grown-up."

Her response made me feel even more abandoned. It must be true; my own family did not want me back. They had seen what life could be without me and preferred it that way. My heart was broken, and I felt miserably alone. The little girl in me just wanted her mommy to make it all better.

I discovered this excerpt on a blog written by Sara Roizen, art therapist and adoptee. She quotes Nancy Verrier's book *The Primal Wound*.

"What adoptees need to know is that their experience was real. Adoption isn't a concept to be learned, a theory to be understood, or an idea to be developed. It is a real-life experience about which adoptees have had and are continuing to have constant and conflicting feelings, all of which are legitimate. Their feelings are their response to the most devastating experience they are ever likely to have: the loss of their mother. Just because they do not consciously remember it does not make it any less devastating. It only makes it more difficult to deal with, because it happened before they had words with which to describe it (preverbal) and is, therefore, almost impossible to talk about. For many of them, it is even more difficult to think about. In fact, some adoptees say they feel as if they either came from outer space or a file drawer. To allow themselves the memory of being born, even a feeling sense of it, would mean also having to remember and feel what happened next. And that they most certainly do not want to do that" (Roizen, 2009).

This blog and quote felt validating!

My adoptive mother's rejection of my request to come home hit me like a ton of bricks. I was not fully aware how deeply that cut until much later in my life. Resilience is a quality I learned at an early age. I usually brushed myself off and kept going, despite the hurt and pain I felt on the inside. I suspected things could be different but was not able to challenge it. All I really wanted was to be accepted and to belong.

My dad called me the next day to tell me I could come home anytime I wanted. Remember how I said he made me feel safe? That was consistent. He was the only one who could stand up to my mother, and he always protected me.

I applied and was accepted to Flagler College. I quit my job, got rid of all my belongings, and was ready to embark on my new journey. I was petrified, uncertain, and still in crisis as this change came to life.

THE BIGGEST DISRUPTION AND BETRAYAL

A month before my twenty-fifth birthday, I left the only place I had ever known and moved to St. Augustine, Florida. I started college right away and attended classes with eighteen- and nineteen-year-old students. I missed my New York life and all my friends immensely. I was afraid I would be forgotten, or worse, dumped again. I reminded myself, *You are not fourteen, AnnMarie. You have control over your choices, and you chose to move here and complete your degree. Yes, you made that choice after your live-in boyfriend cheated on you. You felt betrayed and abandoned.* I was still trying to find the place where I belonged.

My next challenge was to find my place back in the family. I had been living on my own as an adult for six years. In the meantime, my family, including my adoptive brother and sister who were nine and six years younger, had been building a new life and a new family dynamic—one that did not include me. I was staying in my parents' house, a home in which I had never lived. I was trying to connect with teenage siblings who had grown up without me during their formative years. It all felt a bit much.

I didn't have any place where I felt settled or part of something. I was an outsider at school and at home.

Flagler turned out to be a place where I made lifelong friends, but that had not transpired yet. In that moment, I was isolated and incredibly lonely. One evening, I was chatting with my mom.

She said, "You know I am really glad you are here. I have so many things I want to talk to you about, things I want to tell you."

I looked her straight in the face and said, "Oh really? Like what? That I'm adopted?"

She stared back and replied, "Well, actually, yes."

Panic overcame me, physically, emotionally, and mentally. I sat there in disbelief. *Was this a cruel joke? Come on, Mom. That's not funny.*

Somewhere in what seemed to be a far distance I heard her say, "There were so many times we wanted to tell you but the timing was not right."

Talk about identity annihilation. How could I be adopted? None of it made sense. One thing was clear as day: I had climbed another rung on the abandonment ladder. Problem was the ladder was not taking me anywhere useful.

My head was reeling. So many scenarios to evaluate and sentiments swirling around. Think bubbles with words above them as if in a comic strip. Thoughts just taunting me: *You don't belong, see? Neither of your families wanted you. That's why you don't fit in here. Do you even fit in anywhere? Why are you here?*

My mother tried to explain how it all came to be and why she waited until now.

"I wanted to tell you on your sixteenth birthday, but I didn't think you were ready."

"I wanted to tell you when you graduated high school, but we found out we were moving."

That one was a good call on her part.

"I wanted to tell you recently, and then you and your boyfriend broke up."

What about all the time leading up to my sixteenth birthday? Looking back, I understand why she felt it was hard to find the right time to tell me, especially since we were in crisis most of the time. I felt there were some distinct times when knowing I was adopted could have benefited me. At this moment, when my life was already in complete disruption, this felt like absolutely the wrong time. Nobody truly wanted me. I was not connected to any single human I knew.

She did not share any specific details about my adoption that night. We focused mainly on all the reasons why she waited so long to tell me. I needed time to process before I asked questions and sought further details.

ABANDONMENT COULD BE FOUND EVERYWHERE
The theme of abandonment continued throughout my adult life. I realized how I've fed the story like a hungry animal, keeping it alive and living in complete and utter fear of it. Abandonment came in many forms.

One of my relationships was with a partner who had dabbled in drugs and had issues with the law. During our two-and-a-half-year relationship he was arrested twice. The first time he stole a computer from the company we both worked for, and I got fired. I gave him another chance. About a year and half later we got pulled over for a broken taillight and he was taken away by state troopers for an outstanding warrant.

Good people sometimes make poor decisions. However, this was not how I wanted to live.

Another one of my relationships started while I was on vacation with my girlfriends. I met a guy who turned out to be on the run from the law. I disregarded the red flag and proceeded to cultivate a relationship with him. He moved to New York City and lived with me. I knew we had no future but I still dated him for a couple of years. He turned himself in eventually, to turn his life around. He told me I was the catalyst for that decision. We kept in touch and wrote letters. In hindsight, his incarceration was another form of abandonment.

I habitually attracted and chose physically and emotionally unavailable men. As I examined my relationship patterns it became clear: I tolerated certain behavior from others because those circumstances felt safer, and it was all I believed I was worthy of. Ultimately, I would have a reason to leave them before they left me.

I constructed similar barriers in work situations. I'd been fired from several jobs. I played into the story of abandonment through the choices I made and the behavior I accepted from others. I was not a victim in any of these situations. I was an active participant.

During these incidents, I felt like these things were happening to me. I was anchored to the belief that change needed to be precipitated by crisis. I attracted crisis! I had not figured out another way to attract different types of people and create better outcomes. Neither of these people are bad. I know where both are today and they are doing very well. They served a significant part in my story and my journey. I take full responsibility for my role in their lives and the stories we cocreated at different points in our lives.

A SENSE OF FREEDOM EMERGED
Finding out I was adopted introduced a sense of freedom.

The prior story I hung on to was: "I came from a family where I don't fit in, and people didn't appreciate me."

This new information filled in some of the gaps about myself and my feelings of not belonging. It shined a light on the belief I carried around that something was wrong with me. My instincts turned out not to be wrong. Something was askew.

I had felt abandoned before I fully understood how it all began. My biological mother didn't want me or couldn't keep me. That felt like the ultimate abandonment. Yet learning this was a relief at the same time. I wasn't as broken as I had convinced myself. Nothing was wrong with me because I felt detached or like I did not belong.

As I've done research and spoken with other adoptees, I've realized everyone's story is different. I have discovered many accounts of adoptees who share similar experiences to mine. They also felt like they did not fit in.

The abandonment story did not end here.

As I wrote the book, I understood how active this abandonment story still was in my life. My adoptive mom always said I was born from her heart and she needed me. She said having me saved her. I wanted to believe her, but her behavior didn't always match her words. I didn't know about being born from her heart until I was an adult. The childhood version of me relied on her behaviors and the words she used. She often accused me of selfishness. She berated my weepy, pissy-eyed existence.

Once those beliefs were instilled, I could not just wake up one day and say, "Everything is fine now."

I don't know the story of why she decided to adopt me. I think she thought she couldn't bear her own children, but she ultimately ended up having two biological kids after she had me.

I spent time working through all my abandonment stories. I recognized I easily allowed how others treated me to represent who I was instead of learning to see, accept, and embrace the good in me. I never had the freedom to embrace my true self. When that version didn't match others' expectations, I conformed.

Finding out I was adopted introduced a whole new set of data to interpret and recalibrate into my life.

Fortunately, I met teachers, friends, bosses, and coaches who saw and acknowledged characteristics of mine that were not welcomed or encouraged before. After doing the work, I trust my mother's words. I know she meant it. I was a gift in her life. I was a good daughter. I did my best to show up for her. I was always trying to understand myself better. I have the tools to see things from her perspective when we conflicted.

My adoptive mom passed away suddenly on February 28, 2023. Thankfully, we were in a good place, and I attribute my personal growth to the pivot that occurred within our relationship.

When those demons who plague or taunt me show their ugly head, I know I am not those stories of abandonment. They are thoughts and don't define me. I make choices based on what is best for me, not so others will include me or not abandon me.

The biggest lesson I've learned is abandoning myself is far worse than being abandoned by anyone else.

CHAPTER 3

ADOPTED BIRDS OF A FEATHER

Growing up, adoption was not a forbidden topic in our family. My adoptive mom's sister adopted her two sons and it was openly discussed as were growing up. The thought that sprung to mind when I learned my backstory was, *How come my cousins were worthy of knowing their birth status but I was lied to about mine?*

I asked my mom, "I knew my cousins were adopted. Why did you think it would be difficult for me to learn I was as well?"

She didn't have a good answer. It's still confusing. She thought the two situations were completely unrelated. I felt she could not trust me to handle the truth and didn't believe I was capable.

Neither of my cousins ever had any interest in finding their biological families, which, in my opinion, made it more difficult to be truthful about my desire to find mine. I felt selfish for wanting to know more.

ADOPTEES SHARE COMMON STRUGGLES
Adoptee blogger Pamela A. Karanova shares her viewpoint.

As a young girl, Pamela learned she was adopted, and she was told her biological mother loved her "so much" she gifted her to another woman to care for her. Becoming a mother was this other woman's dream come true, so there was no room left for Pamela's sadness regarding this news (Karanova 2014).

These words mirrored how I felt about my need to search and the possibility of hurting my adoptive mom. How can I break the heart she told me I was born from by being curious about my biological parents, especially my biological mother? This is a great example of how I bury my own desires to protect other people.

Pamela also shares her philosophy, "When adoptees don't have their truth, healing is unachievable" (Karanova 2014).

That was true for me and ultimately pushed me to the brink of my search. It was the only way for me to be able to truly heal the deep abandonment wounds.

ADOPTED SOUL SISTERS
In addition to my two cousins, I have a few friends who are adopted.

I met Laurie the year I moved back to New York, after college graduation. The news of my adoption was still fresh, and I was very vulnerable as I tried to assimilate this new information into my life. My emotions were raw, and the confusion

I felt about all of it was very visceral. Laurie provided a safe space for me and supported me while I processed it. Laurie was so open about her adoption experience. She knew her birth mom and shared the details with me. She was the first person to fully understand what I was grappling with, and she made the subject way less taboo. The freedom to own the adoption part of my story was unearthed through my friendship with her.

I recently reconnected with Laurie. The opportunity to share how our respective journeys affected us and played out further into our adult lives has been such an incredible gift for me. We picked up where we left off, and I was again reminded how meaningful it was to have her guidance and friendship thirty years earlier.

My friend Nicole and I have known each other since the second grade. For as long as I can remember, I've known her entire family. We all grew up knowing Nicole and her younger brother Joseph were adopted. Nicole's parents had an incredibly welcoming and inclusive nature. They extended their hearts and their already large biological family when they adopted Nicole and Joseph. What I didn't know then, or even until quite recently, was she would be a guide in my journey.

Did you ever meet someone and feel instantly drawn or connected to them but not fully able to understand or articulate why? That's been my relationship with Nicole since we were eight years old. She has been in and out of my life over these last five decades.

We met in the second grade, the same year I actually started to remember my school experiences. Nicole and I ended up back in class together for seventh and eighth grade. Her friend group is the one that took me into their fold in Franklin K. Lane after I had been abandoned by my friend group. Our friendship strengthened from there. We dated brothers. Neither of us married either of them, yet we still fondly refer to each other as sisters-in-law.

We are soul sisters. Our adoption bond might be an invisible cord that has kept us linked throughout most of lives, even though our adoption circumstances and stories are so drastically different.

We stayed in touch after high school, and then started to drift apart. I told myself life took us in different directions. I disengaged, which is another pattern I identified as I was healing and learning more about my patterns.

In 1998 I started my own company, and we had a client in White Plains. One day I ran into Nicole in the elevator. She worked in the same building. That was serendipitous. It was so great to reconnect, though life and other factors caused us to lose touch again for another ten years.

Thankfully, we once again found each other, and have been in consistent contact since then. I know we could both benefit from more engagement, but we do our best. I absolutely treasure our time together. She reflects the type of friend I want to be. Nicole is incredibly loyal and inclusive.

I've been watching her search story unfold. She generously shared her experiences and feelings about her journey. In 2018, Nicole connected with one of her maternal siblings, her younger brother. Over the past five years, she has united with her paternal family. Her parents are deceased, but she has met siblings, nieces, nephews, aunts, and cousins. She has developed strong relationships with some of them.

When I met her brothers, I could see the resemblance, both physical and through mannerisms they had in common. In her younger brother, I see Nicole's smile and her eyes. Her older brother embodies the same natural friendliness and inclusivity Nicole has demonstrated her whole life.

She shared with me how happy her older brothers are to have a baby sister. They accepted and embraced her. Her story is not without family drama, but she shows up and deals with things as they arise. I am so happy for her. She became the catalyst for me to question why I had not pursued my own search.

Why am I sitting on the sidelines? Can't I see how rich this experience has been for her? Don't I long to meet my biological siblings? What am I afraid of?

Nicole was aware of my reluctance and fear of looking for my biological family. She also understood I had a deep yearning to know more about my roots. She always offered to help me when I was ready.

She generously reminded me, "I know it's scary, but I am here for you. We can do this together."

I chose to be a spectator on her journey as opposed to making any movements in mine, which felt confusing. I am not generally indecisive or scared to act, but the stakes in this situation were incredibly high. Also, when Nicole's story started to evolve, I was in the process of selling my twenty-year tech business. I gave myself grace and acknowledged timing plays a significant role in major life decisions.

Watching Nicole locate, connect with, and form a relationship with her biological family has been very inspiring for me. She played a major role in my desire and courage to move forward.

Fifteen years ago, Nicole was contacted by an investigator, Pamela Slaton, who advised she was trying to find Joseph. She was working with his biological sister who hoped to meet him. Nicole was caught off guard by this, but she agreed to take the initial call. Through this we met Sarah, Joe's biological sister.

Nicole, in her usual nature, integrated Sarah into our lives and her family. That was my first actual experience in witnessing a biological family reunion. I remember meeting Sarah and thinking how brave she was. She sought to find her biological family and wanted it so badly she was willing to engage an investigator. I had no way of knowing I would hire the same investigator to find my biological family.

We sadly lost Joseph in November 2020, and continuing to have Sarah in our lives is so special. I have had many conversations with both Nicole and Sarah about finding our biological origins and what that means to each of our respective journeys. They have been incredibly supportive.

A GUIDE TO MY FUTURE

In late 2019, I took a coaching course. My second class was taught by a woman named Deanna. Remember that instant connection I described with my friend Nicole? I felt that with Deanna, as if we'd known each other before or were destined to meet in this lifetime.

Deanna was an IT project manager—wait, *I* was an IT project manager, and now I am a coach! I think this is what synchronicity looks like. I had no idea the parallels between Deanna and I ran far deeper than the IT project manager connection.

Deanna is a beacon of light for me, paving the way as I encounter lots of new, unchartered territory. She continually shines light into dark and scary places I would otherwise avoid. We are the same age, born only about five weeks apart—she's older! Over the past three years, Deanna has been a teacher, coach, mentor, group leader, and guide for me. She is adopted, and we have eerily similar experiences in our respective journeys.

Deanna is the reason I took the leap to write this book. She has this beautiful way of opening doors and cleaning the muck off the windows, so I can see clearly and move toward my dreams. She has a special gift for helping me see myself through an incredibly different lens. I often refer to Deanna as my soul sister. I know we are connected at a soul level. She is a beautiful reminder of how guided and protected I am. When I am open to guidance and listening to what is best for me, magic occurs.

During a workshop Deanna led in early 2020, she shared she had sought to find her biological mom and had sent her a letter. Her bravery inspired me on a cellular level. I was not alone in the experience of seeking to find answers, and there was no "right" time to start.

I also started to believe I belong. It was clear to me I could choose who to surround myself with. I did not have to just show up the way people expected me to. I recognized most of the expectations of others were driven by their own lack and insecurities. This does not mean the friendships and relationships I had fell away. Quite the contrary, I showed up in a new way, which meant most of my relationships strengthened.

EVERYONE'S STORY IS UNIQUE
Whenever I was comfortable enough to share the story of my adoption with others, I often discovered they have a story too. For some, I know they have experience with adoption. Other times, I have no idea. Almost everyone has a story, either about themselves or about someone close to them, that involves a mystery around biological origin. This expands beyond adoption and can include biological estrangement of a parent or siblings.

I have a very close friend who adopted a daughter from another country in 2007. When I shared I found my biological roots, she asked me to tell her daughter. I obliged. Afterward my friend asked her daughter if she had any yearning to find her own family, and she replied she had zero desire.

I was speaking with another friend on the same topic, and she told me her about her two adopted cousins, who were siblings through adoption and not biologically.

Her male cousin found his family, and it turned out (as shared by my friend) he was the spitting image of his father, who had passed away. When he reunited with his biological family, they experienced some very deep reactions. Now they had a new relative who reminded them of someone they had loved dearly and lost.

Her female cousin had no desire to find her family, much like my friend's daughter. However, through a series of events she connected with her biological siblings and eventually with her biological mom. Initially her mom was not ready to meet her—precisely my darkest fear. In her case, once her mother was able to reconcile the idea, they eventually met.

Her mom was married to the father of her siblings, who were born after she gave my friend's cousin up for adoption. He knew about the baby she had to give away when she was a young girl. Every year on her daughter's birthday he took her out for a special lunch to celebrate the life she had brought into this world, even though she was not raising her.

Hearing this story, I was emotionally overwhelmed by this beautiful gesture. Instead of allowing her to sit in shame and guilt, he did his best to celebrate and recognize her daughter, even though she was not in her life.

I was deeply touched by this and it spurred some considerations for me. *Did my biological mom have any special tradition to mark my birthday each year? Did she even think of me on my birthday? Did she even remember the day? Or was I a dark, terrible secret that reminded her of an awful time in her life? Did she just want to erase any presence or thought of me from her life?*

THE SHAME WE CARRY
I've come to learn shame or guilt is typically attached to adoption. I felt guilty for wanting to find them. I felt shame that I was rejected.

I imagine my biological mother carries shame. As I can only control my piece of this, I chose to let go of guilt and fear of further rejection. The choice to let go and surrender felt like freedom.

I am curious about those who say they have no desire to find their biological families. I wonder if they are potentially disconnected from their true feelings. Is there a fear of something else that makes them dismiss the need to know more about how their story came to be? I would venture to guess it's either just not the right timing or they're not being completely honest with themselves.

This is purely my opinion, and I recognize this is a sensitive subject. A journey of self is specifically individual, and timing is undeniably critical. For many years, I was ambivalent about my adoption story and avoidant about the topic of searching for my biological family. I now understand that was my defense mechanism, aiming to protect me from further rejection and betrayal.

What I didn't understand was this armor I had built caused more damage than protection. I blocked myself from honest, true, and deep connection. I assumed everyone would treat me the way I had been treated. I believed I was destined for a lifetime of disappointment and heartbreak.

I had proof from other adoptees in my life as well as other true friends and my husband that I could attract good people who love me for who I am. It was still hard for me to truly believe I was lovable or worthy of deep and lasting relationships. I was on a journey of learning and claiming my identity.

Our actions undeniably affect others, even when our intentions are good.

I wonder who truly owns the details of a child's birth: the parents or the child? A parent can make an argument they are acting in the child's best interest by not telling them the details because they want to protect them. My adoptive mother wanted to protect me.

A child can argue they have every right to know their origin story, even if it may be painful for the people who are involved. I am not a parent, so I can only comment on this through the lens of my experience as a child who was lied to for twenty-five years.

THE PIECES OF OUR STORIES

Humans are built on a foundation of stories: the stories they created themselves, the stories created for them, and the stories they cocreated and continue to cocreate with others. The struggle is we've convinced ourselves the stories define who we are, and we can't rewrite them. We bring characters into versions of stories that don't even exist. We even go so far as to write scripts for those characters who are out of alignment with their own actual stories, urging them to stay part of our plot.

I find myself trying to justify to others why I needed to search, especially since I avoided it for so long. When I watched an Oprah special about the reunion between a biological mother and her daughter, Oprah said, "You can't find peace until you find the missing piece" (Winfrey, 2010).

I started crying, almost uncontrollably. That's a profound and impactful way to describe the adoptee experience. I felt incredibly validated hearing her speak those words out loud.

I used to try and justify this by saying, "It is not necessarily that something is actually missing but I feel like it is."

To be perfectly clear, something is missing. The woman who carried me in her womb was gone after I was birthed. This is not meant to be a negative reflection on any of the people who are, or are not, in my life. It is the reality.

Adoption conjures up many emotions for everyone involved. My responsibility is to myself, yet I find myself apologizing or making excuses because I want to know more. This was another lesson that kept coming up for me. I cannot be responsible for how other people react to my decisions. My intention is not to bulldoze anyone's feelings—not my adoptive mom, or my biological mother, or any others who would be affected if I shared my truth.

Instead, I've done the opposite. I've held back what I want so others wouldn't get hurt. I can't do that any longer. *What would my life be, if at the end of it I was all bottled up with the things I never said, did, or felt? How would I feel if I spent my entire existence protecting others at the expense of not living my life the way I wanted?*

Thoughts like these could be interpreted as selfish, but I have learned starting with self is the absolute best way to live.

Many decisions were made about my life. Even if these were all made with good outcomes in mind, my feelings were not considered. By not going for what I want, my feelings are still not considered, but this time I am the culprit.

Maybe not all adoptees feel this way, but I do. I don't know exactly how my biological mother felt when she gave me up or what my mom experienced when she adopted me. I won't try to pretend I understand. I know my feelings, and it is my right to embrace them and to speak the truth about how I was affected.

Finding all the pieces was important for me. *What traits do I have from my biological family? Who do I resemble? Was I named after someone?*

Finding my biological roots seemed more attainable than it ever had been. Before I began my search, I had no idea how things would unfold and no expectations or attachments to what would be. I trusted my intuition and guidance, especially when I had the privilege to hear the stories of others. I embraced the support that was offered while I embarked on my own courageous journey.

Finding my biological family has zero impact on the facts. My adoptive mom is my mom. I have many attributes and characteristics that are direct results of how I was raised and not how I was born. I have my adoptive mother's resilience, her tenacity, and her people-pleasing tendencies. Sometimes when I hear myself speaking, I can hear my adoptive mom's voice. She taught me how to stand up for myself and that someone else was always in a worse position. That was her way of expressing gratitude. I am grateful she chose me and raised me. I am not looking to rewrite that part of my story.

While I was writing this book, I shared the above paragraph with my mom. She responded, "I love when you share. It's very healing."

One woman birthed me. One woman raised me. Thanks to those experiences, I am who I am today. I embrace all the pieces of my story.

CHAPTER 4

THE DNA DANCE

If I just complained about being controlled, lied to, or abandoned, and did not do anything differently, history would be converted to the present and the cycle repeated. The negative aspects are just one part. While my story has had many cocreators and influencers, where I take it from here is fully up to me. No more blaming, no more shaming, and no more excuses or avoidance. I own whatever ramifications arise as I move forward.

I chose to speak my truth and tell my story.

Though I found out I was adopted as a young adult, it took time for reality to sink in. It was hard for me to reconcile my mother's rationale for keeping the secret. She was afraid of how it would impact me. This felt like a contradiction since the time she picked to tell me was when I had totally disrupted my life with a big change. She opted to spring this on me the first week I arrived, as opposed to giving me some time to settle in before dropping such an emotional bomb. Perhaps she believed my life was already in shambles, and this couldn't make it any worse.

Chaos was where she thrived, and this was certainly a chaotic time. When I pressed the issue of why she decided to speak the truth then, my mother revealed where her urgency was coming from. My sister found out I was adopted. She was afraid my sister would tell me and that would have an even more profound effect on me. The theme in my family is most change came through crisis, so this played perfectly into that established dynamic. If my mother didn't tell me first, my sister would find a way to drop it on me in an argument or as a dagger.

When I got the news, I was in no position to consider finding my biological family. I had just quit my job, given up my own home in New York City, left all my friends, and started college full time. I let this new information simmer and seep in. This was not the time to act. I needed time to process.

THE DEAD-END SEARCH ATTEMPT

About five years later, after I graduated college and moved back to New York, I was ready to look for them. I was thirty and thought, if I was going to have children and even for my own medical knowledge, I should know more about my genetics and family history. My friend Jennifer offered to help. I agreed and asked her to call the hospital where I was born to get a copy of my birth records.

The response to her inquiry was, "We are sorry, but after thirty years all records are archived."

I told her not to worry. I had the papers from the lawyer and contacted them. My assumption was the lawyer's office that handled the adoption had my biological parents' information.

When I first moved back to New York, my mom came to visit. She brought the adoption records, which had my birth name, Geri Lynn Jackman. That was the first time I learned the name I had been given at birth. It was surreal, and still is to some extent, to have a totally different name at birth, just to have it changed when my adoptive parents stepped in. I had not given it much thought, but I wondered why my mom hadn't given me those papers while I was still living in Florida.

I struggled thinking of myself as anyone else. Geri Lynn seemed like a ghost to me, yet she is me. A part of me wanted to believe that maybe this was just all a big misunderstanding. Having those adoption papers in my hand, and seeing my birth name, was conclusive evidence. This was, in fact, very real. I experienced an identity crisis and questioned so many things. It took twenty-five more years to reconcile the identity fusion between Geri Lynn and AnnMarie.

When I called the lawyer's office, I explained my situation to the lady who answered the phone. She hesitated and asked if someone could get back to me. I obliged. My call was returned promptly. A man explained he was the son of the attorney who handled my adoption thirty years ago. This was a real lead!

He went on to say, "I am sorry, but my dad recently passed away. We are in the process of packing up all the records."

He did not seem interested in participating in my search. I didn't push back. This was another dead end. Literally.

I have a philosophy that things work out as they are supposed to. When impassable obstacles arose, I took it as a sign that this was not the right time. I had just started a new business and told myself it was better not to open a potential can of worms. I had a lot going on, and this could have been a great distraction. I abandoned my search and went about life.

A CASE OF THE WHAT-IFS
The years passed, I got busy with growing the company, and then I met my husband and kept moving through life. The topic of my search came up a few times while we were planning our wedding.

Each time it came up I responded, "It's probably not the right time."

In my mind I rationalized as the what-ifs swirled in my head. *What if they are crazy? What if they didn't want anything to do with me?* Considering what might be waiting on the other side felt overwhelming. I had no control of that part.

I also didn't want to hurt my adoptive mother. *Would she feel betrayed? Would she feel like she was losing me?* It was complicated and not worth the pursuit.

What I didn't understand was how this was affecting me. This unknown part of my life influenced my thoughts and my decisions, reinforcing the abandonment story I had been telling myself and living.

In 2007 I married Anderson. This was the same year 23andMe was founded. Ancestry.com had been around since 1983 and started as a publishing house. Services like this opened a whole new realm of possibilities. I recall Oprah Winfrey featured reunions of adoptees and their biological families. For a moment I thought this was a sign to reengage in my search. Instead, I told myself the timing still didn't fit. Even though more resources were available now, I did not feel emotionally ready for the efforts it would take nor how my life could potentially be affected. I remained afraid and let that fear decide.

I had a lot going on. We were busy planning a wedding. Anderson comes from a very large family, which is wonderful. They accepted and embraced me, and it was such a beautiful time, I didn't want to do anything that would invite crisis.

My business also required focus and attention. I was worried about the disturbance finding them would cause, especially at a time when things were finally going well. Each time I considered searching for my biological family, I told myself, *I am too busy, and my life is in a good place.* The what-ifs were still loud and scary. It felt too daunting.

In retrospect, I was paralyzed by the potential of more rejection or learning what I had missed. *What if they were this wonderful family and they were all close and connected? I would once again find myself outside looking in, not fitting in or feeling accepted.*

Deep down, I knew I was not ready to handle that. I kept busy and distracted to avoid thinking about searching for my biological family. I wonder if this was like what my mom did when she kept putting off telling me about the adoption?

In 2017, I turned fifty and was reminded time is finite. Each year, month, week, or day that passed without making any effort was time I could not regain. I was increasingly aware of the gap in my life. I thought about the missing piece of my puzzle, just as Oprah had said.

NO MORE EXCUSES

In 2018, I bought the DNA kits and started with 23andMe. The service had been available for quite some time. Maybe the timing was finally right. That kit sat on the coffee table in the living room, in plain sight, and each day I ignored it. I would sort through the mail and just shuffle the box out of the way. Anderson gently reminded me and offered to set it up.

My consistent reply: "No, not today."

And then I provided a list of excuses, such as "I'm busy. I am not sure how long it will take."

I waited so long that when we finally opened it, the kit had dried up, which felt like a perfect metaphor for this entire experience. Nothing good could come of this.

My reaction was, "Oh well, there's sixty dollars down the drain."

Anderson was not giving up that easily. He called the company and they sent a replacement. In July 2018, I finally swabbed, and we mailed it. I also decided to do Ancestry. I had taken the first step.

I felt vulnerable. We waited to see what matches came across. I was not consistent in checking the updates. Waiting was uncomfortably overwhelming. At this writing, I have no sibling or parent matches on either site. The matches were mostly distant cousins, second, third, and fourth cousins, scattered everywhere.

It was a very odd experience because I had no idea if Jackman was my mother or father's name. I had no idea how I was connected to any of these people. *Were they my maternal or paternal cousins? Were their parents my cousins, or one of my parents' cousins? How did I fit into their family tree?* I felt awkward and left out, again. These people knew their biological roots. They were not using this tool to try and find out where they came from, so it was a different exercise for me.

A DNA MATCH IGNITES FORWARD MOVEMENT
In 2020 something happened that gave me hope. A woman named Cathy contacted me. She was researching her mom's family and believed her mom and I were possibly first cousins. Her mom was a Jackman, but they did not have much information about that side of the family. She lived in California, so I found myself a little leery at first. *How could I be related to someone who lived in California?* I was conflicted. At the same time, I felt drawn to her. Something about her felt trustworthy.

We communicated via the DNA app at first, and then we moved to email. She eventually sent me a Facebook friend request, which I avoided accepting. *Why was I avoiding it? Isn't this what I wanted?*

She was approachable, patient, kind, and potentially a biological family member! Yet I kept her at arm's distance and didn't engage. I was held back by fear. It is one thing to say you want something and another to have it. You can feel incredibly unsure about what to do next and end up doing nothing.

In 2021, I took a sabbatical, a monthlong road trip that started in Grand Haven, Michigan, and took me through Michigan's Upper Peninsula, Minnesota, Wisconsin, North Dakota, and Montana. The second part of the trip was in southern California, and I realized I would be relatively close to where Cathy lived. I reached out to her and offered to meet in person. She was receptive and we coordinated the time.

My sabbatical was meant to be an exploratory experience. I intentionally took time away from my day-to-day hustle to truly consider what was next, both professionally and personally. I considered it a journey for myself, to quiet the outside expectations and get clear on what I wanted.

During this trip I finally accepted the big missing puzzle piece. Not knowing my origin story had a profound impact on my ability to truly heal. Those lingering questions that remained unanswered flashed like neon lights in a dark room where I could never fully rest. *Where do I come from? Who do I look like?* I finally felt like I had space to dig into this. *Why was I not doing the work? Why was I not prioritizing the search for my family? Was it time to finally face these fears?*

The meeting with Cathy and her husband Joe was two days before I headed back to New York. I had a moment where I thought we were going to cancel. She lived over an hour away from where I was staying. My friend and I discussed the Sunday traffic, and it seemed to be too much effort. I abruptly started crying. I guess I do cry a lot! I really wanted to meet her and thought it would be a missed opportunity if we didn't go. My tears gave me information. This was a sign I was ready.

Traffic was terrible, and the drive took us a lot longer than originally anticipated. I received a stressful call from work on the way, which added to the intensity of the drive. I was very anxious and was stewing that I had made my friend feel guilty to agree to take me. My emotional state was raw and shaky.

Cathy picked the place, and she sent me a text to say they had a table outside. The parking lot was full, prolonging the stress and anxiety as we circled looking for a spot. Once we finally parked, the anticipation of meeting her hit me like a ton of bricks. *What if it's awkward? Of course, it will be awkward! What will we talk about? I guess we will talk about me, my adoption, and the fact I know nothing about my biological family.*

We arrived at the table. They had drinks, and her husband informed us it was bottomless mimosas and sangria. I let out a huge sigh of relief and thought, *Perfect! That will help!* We sat down and started chatting. Cathy referred to me as family as she shared a story about "our" cousin.

She said, "I saw that you went to Flagler College. Our cousin went there, and so did her daughter. Isn't that a funny coincidence?"

My heart felt full, and I experienced something previously unknown to me. It was a familiar knowing. I assumed this is what biologically connected family members feel all the time.

She had a folder she had created for me, which was kind, generous, and incredibly thoughtful of her. The folder contained ancestry details about the Jackman family tree. She provided the historical background that Jackman was shortened from Giacomino. The folder included a family photo of the Jackmans dating back to 1908. It was cool to receive this, and I truly appreciated the time and effort she had put in.

Cathy had a few potential inklings about who my parents could have been. She was very concerned about being wrong and didn't want to lead me on or get my hopes up. I appreciated how caring she was with my heart. None of the contents of the folder got us any closer, and we did not solve anything that day. Yet this was a huge step forward. Even though we still don't know exactly how we are related, I have a blood relative. This was my first biological connection. Meeting Joe and Cathy was an incredible gift and I am so thrilled we found each other. We are in touch, and she continues to be so supportive. I value her immensely.

That said, I did not initially handle that gift well. When I got back to New York, I barely kept in touch. I was riddled with fear, avoidance, and thoughts and doubts that were shouting at me, "What's the point?"

TIMING MADE A DIFFERENCE

I resumed my busy lifestyle and put her aside as I had done in the past and as my mom did during the years she didn't think it was a good idea for me to know yet.

What was different this time, though, was I was working on myself. I once again pondered, *Why am I so stuck? What am I resisting? What am I afraid of? How can I clear these blocks?*

I had tools, resources, and a support system. I took a different approach. I forgave myself for not making moves sooner. I gave myself grace for the stalling tactics I employed while I was waiting for the right time. I recognized this was a big deal and maybe the right time had not yet arrived. I started to trust myself more and held myself accountable. If I truly wanted to know my background or find my biological family, I had to work at it, both internally and externally.

LEANING ON OTHERS HELPED ME

In May 2022, I was ready to take big leaps. The first step was to get a copy of my preadoption birth certificate. Nicole told me she would be with me every step.

I reached out to her and said, "Okay, let's do this. I need to send away for my birth certificate."

True to her word, she walked me through the process. When we completed the request, I received a message that my original birth certificate would arrive around September 2, 2022. Perfect! That gave me all summer to muse on the possibilities and prepare for the roller coaster of emotions that, no doubt, would greet me when it came. I anticipated what it would be like to finally have information such as my mother's name, my actual birth date and time, and hopefully my father's name.

In June, I had been traveling for a few weeks. When I returned home, I had a stack of mail to sort. The morning of June 10 I tackled the pile. I spotted an official-looking envelope with red lettering on the outside. It was my birth certificate! How could that be? Hmmm, was this a sign the timing was right?

As I opened the envelope, a wave of emotions came over me. This was proof and not a dream or a cruel joke. I had the adoption papers, but my birth mother's name was not on them, so it didn't feel as real. My mother's name was on the birth certificate, and it was the same last name that was on my adoption papers, but I didn't know if it was her maiden name or married name. A father was not listed on the birth certificate, another dead end.

I stared at that blank line and felt the deep absence of not knowing who my father was. The omission left a big gap in the story, though I am not sure how knowing his name would have given me any more insight into the situation that occurred fifty-five years earlier. Even without any greater access to the details that led to my adoption, it somehow felt like I'd taken a step closer.

The certificate indicated she had three children before me. It also had my birth time, 4:33 p.m., a previously unknown detail that always bothered me. Knowing what time I was born brought me a settled feeling. I started scouring the internet looking for my mother. Still so many unanswered questions.

Not too long after receiving my birth certificate, a college friend and I were talking and she asked me, "What's going on with your biological family? Are you still planning to try and find them?"

Her question was a little random, but I answered, "Yes, of course, I just don't seem to have enough information though."

She told me about an investigator who had worked with Oprah, and I mentally checked out during the conversation. I thought, *As if I am going to work with someone that's been on Oprah.*

She sent me a link, but I didn't look at it, which was possibly more avoidance on my part.

However, on July 18, I was researching and came across the same investigator she had mentioned to me. I was drawn to her style and ability to make these reunions occur. The work she was doing was deep and meaningful.

Pamela Slaton was the investigator referenced on Oprah, and the one my friend had recommended I check out. Was this a sign? *Were things lining up? Was I ready to continue to move forward?*

Before I could overthink it, I filled out a request form on Pam's site. Her approach was "no find no fee," which I was grateful for because it felt less risky. I believed my case was difficult and finding my mother, father, siblings, and other relatives would be hard. After all, it had been thirty years and I had not gotten far through my own efforts.

Pam contacted me the next day via email and sent me her contract. *Am I really doing this?* When I first received my birth certificate, I had another recommendation for an investigator. I had reached out to her and we exchanged several emails. I didn't feel comfortable with her communication style but, of course, I assumed I was just stalling again. Turned out I was listening to and trusting my instincts. She was not the right fit. I was meant to work with Pam to find my biological family.

Later that same Tuesday night I signed the contract. I discussed it with Anderson, and he agreed I had nothing to lose. Pam called me Wednesday, and we had a lovely conversation. She was originally from Queens, and we clicked.

I told her what information I had (birth certificate and DNA sites) and she said, "No problem, just send me what you have."

Around 1:30 p.m. on Wednesday I sent her the log-on information for my DNA sites and a picture of my birth certificate. I went about my day, assuming I had at least thirty days to prepare. See a theme here?

Thursday evening I was at my office and had a Zoom call scheduled. I needed information to log in, which was in my Gmail account.

When I logged in, I noticed a message from Pam which read, "I have found your biological mom and your three siblings, and I believe I have a paternal match. Here are the details to submit your payment, and I will send you the information."

I sat in sheer disbelief. In thirty hours, she found what took me thirty years to get the courage to look for. Some may call this divine timing. That was not what was going through my head in that moment.

First thought: No way. This is too soon. I am not ready yet. Second thought: That was too easy. I am surely being scammed. Third thought: Damn it, if it was that easy, how come I could not figure it out? Last thought: This is really happening!

CHAPTER 5

BIOLOGICAL LINKS

IT FELT WAY TOO EASY
Was Pam a scammer? After receiving her email, I was filled with anticipation, fear, doubt, and overall angst about the next steps. My brain abruptly switched to dread mode. Life is not this easy. Something must be wrong.

I was still at work and discussed the situation with some of the techs still in the office. How can I protect myself if I paid the fee and she was not legit? What recourse would I have?

I also reached out to a few people to see if they had any knowledge of Pam and her business. Turned out I knew quite a few people who had used her service over the years. Everything came together. Perhaps the timing was right, and it was this easy.

I decided it was best to wait until the next day to pay the fee. Taking a moment to digest the fact I would be receiving long-awaited information about my biological family made sense. The pause was palpable, but the fear of what was waiting for me even more so. I was caught up thinking it was happening way too fast, or perhaps I was just looking for an excuse to avoid yet again. The feedback I received confirmed Pam was legit and reputable.

I had a call with Pam on Friday morning so she could run through the findings before we moved on to the next steps. She asked me if someone had referred me and if it was Sarah. I had totally forgotten she worked with Sarah fifteen years earlier and had contacted Nicole about Joseph. I had not put that together in the midst of what was spiraling in my head. After getting that reminder about Sarah, I called Nicole so we could talk the situation through. True to her word, she was right by my side.

Finally, I summoned the courage to make the payment. I asked Nicole to stay on the phone with me while I hit send.

I texted Pam, "Okay, payment has been made."

She replied, "I am out and will send everything in a few hours."

I exhaled. I had a few hours to prepare for what was coming.

Nicole and I stayed on the phone and speculated about the future. What would Pam's email include? She mentioned she made a paternal match as well. Does that mean she found my father?

Just ten minutes later I received another text from Pam, "Okay, I've sent it."

What? Why does this keep happening? Doesn't the universe know I need time to prepare! I didn't know exactly what I would be doing with that time to prepare, but I believed I needed time to get ready.

WHEN I "MET" MY FAMILY

I told Nicole, "I need you to stay on the phone with me while I open the email and look at this information."

Of course, she complied. When I opened the email, I was greeted with my biological mother's information, picture, Facebook profile, phone numbers, and address. In that moment, I learned she lived only twenty minutes away from me. The email included information about her first husband (my siblings' father) as well as information about all three of my siblings. I had forwarded the email to Nicole, so she saw firsthand what I was looking at.

She exclaimed, "Oh, I knew this person [their father] had something to do with your mother! I saw his name several times on Ancestry.com. We were so close to finding them ourselves."

I had given Nicole my DNA sites' credentials. Even she was not able to put the pieces of the puzzle together. That's why it was so hard to believe Pam was so fast. She is a professional, and this was her expertise. From a zoomed-out perspective, working with her made sense and I am glad I made that decision.

I found myself looking at a picture of my paternal grandmother and a young, handsome man. At first, we thought he was my father. Later we found out he was a family friend. I learned it took time, and a lot of heart, to validate all the provided information. I was once again in a complete state of overwhelm. But this time it was different, it was pure emotional overwhelm. I had information I had dreamed about for so long. I sat with Nicole on the phone, and we talked through each of the findings, especially the photos.

I shared my reactions with her, "I know this is going to sound a bit weird, but I feel so much more connected to my father's family. I look like my grandmother. I can feel her. Does that make any sense to you?"

She validated my sentiments, "Yes, of course. I know exactly how you feel."

When we looked at my mother's Facebook profile photo, Nicole commented, "Oh look, your mother wears pretty jewelry just like you do. You have that in common with her."

My mother had jet-black hair and dark eyes, and so did most of the family, based on the photos I saw. I have light brown hair and brown eyes. Their features were much darker than mine. She has dimples, which are a prominent feature of mine. I searched deeply for more resemblance but fell short. I suppose I always thought when I finally found her, it would be like looking in a mirror. I would instantly have a knowing. That did not happen. The moment was surreal. I had played scenarios in my head about these people, who they were, and how they lived their lives. Now I knew who they were, but they still had no idea I existed. This part of the journey was just beginning.

I recently had a conversation with a friend who was adopted. She never had any desire to find her biological family. At one point, she sent away for nonidentifying information and ended up learning her mother's name. Curiosity is a natural tendency, and she went to Facebook and looked her mother up. In plain sight she saw a photo of a woman with all sorts of knitting apparatus around her.

My friend said, "I was like, oh yes, there I am in another thirty years."

She connected with her mother over Facebook but had not met her in person. She shared she would not pursue that. This exchange provided more evidence that each story and situation is as unique as the individual on their respective journey.

Nicole mentioned she had been doing some research on my roots. We had not discussed her findings until this point. It seemed she was close to identifying some of my close biological family, but because I did not know the last name was my mother's, we were still unclear who we were looking for. The only direct contact I had was Cathy.

Nicole reflected. "I've seen a lot of these names before. I just wasn't sure exactly how they were related to you."

Next, we reviewed the details about my father. He was nineteen years old when I was born and five years younger than my mother. He died when he was twenty-one years old.

Learning this was difficult for me. He died so young. What could have possibly happened to him? Thinking about his life ending so young made me sad. I assumed it was tragic, but we didn't have information yet to corroborate that assumption.

I looked further at the photos Pam provided. The ones of my father's family were older, black-and-white photos. One picture was of my grandfather and my father's oldest sibling, my aunt, when she was a baby. Her daughters are the cousins who generously welcomed me and accepted my invitation to connect. As our relationship progressed, they shared more family photos. The resemblance to my father's family was much more obvious.

The photos of my mother's family were solely from social media, mainly Facebook. I saw the people in her life and got glimpses of their lives. My mother had a large family photo as her cover photo, which I assumed included her grandchildren, my nieces and nephews. They looked like a close and happy family. To me, they were strangers.

When Pam called me to tell me about her findings, she said, "Your mother looks like a lot of fun."

My mother's Facebook profile picture was pretty—she flashed a big, genuine smile and was wearing a long necklace. Hence, Nicole's earlier proclamation about my affinity for costume jewelry and how we had that in common. Talk about stretching to find something to connect us. As I felt with the photo of my grandmother, on my mother's side I felt most connected to her youngest daughter, my older sister. This would be ironic later as the events unfolded.

I did not, in that moment, feel anything for my mother. I started to judge myself for that. But what did I expect to happen? I would see her and recognize her, or feel her love? I suppose I was looking for some sort of familiarity, something deep and profound.

A NEEDED PAUSE TO PROCESS

I left the information for that moment and gave myself space and time to let it all ruminate. I did my best to be incredibly kind to myself. I made sure I maintained a high level of self-care. This was a *big* deal. I tend to underestimate how things affect me, and I wanted to be better about that. This was a great example of how I had learned to give myself what I needed and not repress what I felt. This was a new approach for me and a direct result of my personal growth and the work I had been doing over those past ten years. I didn't have to let this overrun my life in that moment. I had a choice of how to handle all of it.

Two days later, I was finally ready to dig deeper and revisit what I had put aside. Over those two days, I shared the news with some of my closest friends. I recognized I struggled to talk about it. I did not have the words yet for the emotions I was experiencing. Also, exactly how I felt was not fully clear. *Was I excited? Was I relieved? Did I feel differently now that I knew?*

People also had lots of questions, as did I. Problem was I had barely any answers. Some wanted to speculate on how my dad died, and I didn't want to play that game. It was too raw, too new for me to try and guess what might have happened to him. I just found him, and then lost him all in the same day.

I had a busy social weekend planned. I had not expected this to happen so fast. Otherwise, I might have planned some downtime to work through everything. The day I got the email with all the details, I had drinks planned with friends. I did not want to cancel, but I had to be careful because I tend to use alcohol in social situations to numb my feelings or distract me. I stayed mindful, and while I had quite a few drinks, I also checked in with myself the best I could not to allow things to unravel.

The next day we had a bridal shower for one of my best friends' daughters. The plan was to drive with two of my friends, so I knew we would have time in the car for me to share. I did not want to overshadow the shower or make the day about me in any way. I shared a little bit with the two friends I drove with, and then briefly updated my other friend when we arrived. Then we put it away and focused on the day. Being present and in celebration with the bride-to-be and their family was great. I had known the bride since she was born, and her mother since we were teenagers.

Taking control of how I wanted to share the information and putting boundaries in place felt incredibly empowering. The measures I took kept me as grounded as was possible. I did not worry as much as I used to about how people would react when I shared what was going on. This was my story, and I had every right to have it play out how it was most comfortable for me. This was more evidence I had grown and demonstrated to me that waiting until the right time was so critical. All these realizations reminded me why I was not ready before.

NOW THE SCARY PART BEGINS

From the onset it felt safer for me to reach out to my father's family. Maybe because he was deceased, so I didn't have to worry about being rejected or blowing up anyone's life. I decided to contact them first. Also, his family were all my DNA matches on Ancestry. My aunt, his sister, is my highest DNA match. I believe this is how Pam connected the dots that he was my biological father.

His oldest sister had four daughters, and they are all on Facebook. The youngest is my age, just two weeks younger, and we also had mutual friends. Who doesn't love social media? I reached out to one of the mutual friends on Sunday, who assured me my youngest cousin was lovely and encouraged me to contact her.

I waited until Monday and then decided to take a leap and send her a message on Facebook. I wrote:

We are showing as first cousins on Ancestry.com. Since I was adopted, I was not sure how we are related. I have recently learned more about my background and have come to learn who my father is. I believe he was your mom's brother, which makes us first cousins, as Ancestry suggested. I understand your mom has passed recently, and I am truly sorry for your loss and hope it's not too insensitive of me to be reaching out. We do have two mutual friends here. Would you be willing to have a brief phone conversation with me? I am trying to understand a little more about my father's side of the family. He seems to have passed when I was very young (and so was he). I have always wondered about my birth family, and this would be a step for me to learn a little more. Thanks for your consideration. Let me know what would feel best for you.

I got caught up in the excitement after sending that message and called my biological mother next. I left her a voice mail and sent a text. I had not planned to reach out to her yet, but something happened in that moment and I went on the impulse. My messages to her were not as direct. It was more along the lines of:

"I am researching my ancestry, and we show as connected. Would you be willing to have a conversation with me?"

Given how this ended up playing out, I wondered if I should have waited longer. Maybe I should have written a letter to explain more about myself to help them understand who I was and why I was searching now. I think since everything had happened so fast, I got a little swept up in the momentum and took that leap of faith. I did not necessarily think I'd hear back from my mother, but I also wasn't sure what to expect.

My cousin replied within an hour. Her response: "Absolutely. This is crazy." She sent me her phone number.

We chatted that evening. My friend was correct. She was, and still is, lovely and so willing to talk openly with me. I was beyond grateful. She shared that my dad died of leukemia. His illness and death were sudden and tragic for the family. I instantly felt grief and sadness as she shared the story. She was so easy to talk to. She referenced grandma and aunt so-and-so like we were already cousins. Oh wait—we are cousins!

She and her three sisters are very close. She shared how her older sister suggested everyone do Ancestry, and she was building a family tree. I was fascinated by the possibility of knowing more about our family history. We agreed to talk again and invited her sisters and our aunt to join us.

We talked again three days later, on a Thursday. I asked if we could chat via video, and she obliged. Seeing her face was so good. Her sisters were mostly off camera, and our aunt was on speakerphone.

When we shared whatever background information I had received, my aunt said, "If my brother knew she existed, he would have never let her mother give her up."

That filled my heart and made me sad at the same time. For a moment, my mind fluttered with thoughts of how things could have been different if he had known. *What would that mean? What would have happened to me when he passed away?* My heart felt full because I identified with being wanted and not with being abandoned, which is the story I had chosen to believe about my adoption.

SO MANY SPECULATIONS ABOUT HOW AND WHAT COULD HAVE BEEN

It's hard to say which course was better or worse. It does not matter since my life has played out the way it has. It wasn't about comparing to what could have been, it was about understanding how I came to be in this world. I had considerably more information than I ever had. That missing piece finally started to emerge. I did not have all the answers yet, but the details crystalized.

My biological mother lived in an apartment with her three young children, across the hall from my biological grandmother and her kids. My grandfather passed when my dad was young, so he was the man of the house. He was eighteen years old when my mother got pregnant. My aunt did not remember my mother's husband being around, so maybe they had split. I still had so many questions. Identifying the links that connected my birth parents to each other felt incredibly comforting. I still don't know their circumstances. *Did they love each other? How long did their relationship last? Why did she choose not to tell him? Or did she tell him?* Only my mother could answer those questions.

We continued to hunt and discover. My aunt and cousins embraced me. Just one week from when Pam told me she had identified my biological family, I had contact with four cousins and an aunt. I had a better understanding of how my life started. The ease with which this was unfolding almost felt too good to be true, but I soon learned it would not all be that easy.

At one point during my video chat with my cousins, one of her sisters looked at me on the video and said, "She looks just like Grandma."

Another replied, "Oh, she definitely is one of us."

That gave me a sense of belonging I had not ever experienced. I always had this deep yearning to be accepted, included, and part of something. The questions that crossed my mind were, *Who do I look like? Where did I get my dimples from? Did my parents like to write?* The connection biological families seem to share so easily felt elusive to me.

In that moment, I had a glimpse of being included and fitting into a family. Most people experience that because they are born into it. I looked like my grandmother!

Nothing was different. My life had not changed at all—same job, same home, same relationships—yet in one moment everything had altered.

Being seen and accepted by my family was comforting. They were genuinely disappointed they could not help me find more information. They offered to get pictures together and send them to me. And they did just that. One picture was a photo of my father when he was eleven years old. The resemblance between us at that age was undeniable. I have his eyes, both smiling and resting. One of his younger sisters looked exactly like me at that same age. I met her and her son, another one of my cousins, a few months later. She was very emotional and so loving when we met, offering more acceptance. It was beautiful.

These were my biological roots! This was an amazing first step. I felt safe with them, and that matters a lot to me. I felt grateful for their openness and receptiveness.

I felt a greater sense of urgency to try and connect with my biological mother and siblings. Though so many questions were answered, so many new ones emerged. This had all happened so fast with my cousins. In three short days I had connection, photos, and an invitation to keep connecting, which I did and continue to do.

On my mother's side, silence.

CHAPTER 6

NOT ALL STORIES HAVE HAPPY ENDINGS

A COMMON CONTACT

Things were flowing well with my father's family, and I felt my gut instincts were working in my favor. My cousin was very engaged, and she demonstrated a genuine interest in my biological mother's side of the family. I trusted her so I shared what I knew. We were curious if my cousins and siblings had interacted as kids since they all grew up in the same neighborhood.

One evening she called me and said, "My best friend is Facebook friends with your sister."

We had discovered a common link! It was the sister I had originally wanted to reach out to but had hesitated. Without giving it too much thought, I saw this as a sign. We decided my cousin would see what information her best friend might have about my biological mother's side of the family.

I had not made any connection with them yet. I had reached out to my mother but hadn't heard back, so I was not sure if she received the message. I didn't know her circumstances. My intention was not to be invasive, but I felt compelled to keep trying to make contact.

Since I was a stranger to them, they may not have wanted to answer me. When presented with the gift of a mutual connection, I rationalized it might be better coming from someone they trusted.

In hindsight, I realize I had not considered any potential ramifications of sharing personal details with a friend of their family, nor did I think I was overstepping any boundaries. I was caught up by how easily things transpired with my father's family and assumed it was wiser to take this approach. I didn't necessarily expect them to welcome me with open arms, but I hoped my sister would consider a conversation.

My cousin talked to her friend, and she was receptive to the idea. However, she recommended the initial outreach come directly from me. If for some reason my sister didn't respond, then we could leverage her, and she would follow up on my behalf.

I had not considered how my sister would feel about me sharing personal family business with her friends.

I messaged my sister on Facebook: "I've recently discovered some information about my DNA which connects me to the Jackman/Giacomino family. You and I show as a family match, and I am hoping you would be willing to have a conversation with me. I know there are lots of strange messages that fly around Facebook, so you may need more info. Here is my phone number. I was born in Richmond Hill area in 1967, and I still live in Queens. Hoping to hear from you so we can figure out how to best communicate further. Thank you for considering a conversation. I hope we can connect!"

I requested her as a friend in case she wouldn't be able to see the message since we were not Facebook friends. I waited a week and didn't get any response. Based on the message status, it looked like she had not even read it. I checked daily, sometimes a few times a day, continually seeking some sort of acknowledgment.

HINDSIGHT HELD NO VALUE HERE
The more time that passed, I started second-guessing my approach, but it was too late for that. I had already called my mother and sent her a text, and now I was invested in the message I had sent to my sister. I had discussed the situation with her friend, through my cousin. Turning back was not an option. All I needed to do was wait. After a week with no response, I reached out to my cousin to see if we could proceed with the previously agreed upon next steps.

My cousin let me know her friend had reached out to my sister's husband, instead of my sister.

She explained, "After thinking about it more carefully she was a little concerned about how your sister would react, so she contacted her husband to get his thoughts."

Yikes. Maybe we all should have done a little deeper deliberation from the onset. Contact had been made, and they were now aware I existed. I anxiously waited for any recognition or response. *Would she reach out? Would she be willing to talk to me? Would it be as easy as it has been with my father's family thus far?*

I did not have to wait too long.

The next day I received a message back from my sister, which read, "My family and I are not looking to speak with you at this time. Also please refrain from reaching out again, and I would appreciate if you could please stop speaking to my friends or friends of friends about this."

As I read the message, tears fell from my eyes. I didn't even realize I was crying, but her words cut like a knife. This was the message I had been waiting for, but it wasn't the message I wanted to hear.

I promptly replied, "I appreciate you getting back to me, and I respect your decision. I'm adopted and you guys are my biological family. I am not trying to hurt anyone or create any strife. I apologize that I came through your friend. I wasn't sure how else to try and connect. I thought that would be less invasive than me reaching out and blindsiding anyone. I truly do not need anything. I just wanted to meet my biological family. If you ever change your mind or if any of you have any interest in talking to me, I will welcome that."

As I started to type my reply to her, Anderson stopped me and suggested, "Take a breath before you reply."

I answered him, "I know you think I am responding with haste and anger because she rejected me. My intention is to leave the door open for a possible connection in the future. I hope maybe once they've had time to process, they will reconsider."

He listened patiently while I went on to share with him, "The tone of her message triggered me. I thought she lacked any compassion for how I felt in all this. But I am doing my best to rise above it. And yes, I am taking deep breaths. Good reminder."

I never heard back from her. When I caught up with my cousin, she mentioned my sister was really angry I had reached out to her friend.

When her friend prodded her to reply to me, she told her, "I don't need to respond to her. No answer is an answer."

In retrospect, I understand why she was angry. I got caught up in the possibility of meeting them. Even though I had consistently thought about how my mother felt when she gave me up, I didn't really think about how she might feel when I showed up.

I felt immensely sad that the door was shut, but I also felt a glimmer of hope. Her message said, "We are not looking to speak with you **at this time**."

COURAGE AND VULNERABILITY

I hoped once they had time to reconcile this information, they would reconsider. Maybe they never will. Perhaps that call to my sister's husband opened a slew of secrets in their family. My sister could have many reasons for reacting the way she did. I'd crossed a boundary by involving her friend. I owned that in my message back to her. While I was disappointed in her response, I was also proud of myself for going for it.

Author and researcher Brené Brown says, "Vulnerability is not about winning; it's not about losing. It's having the courage to show up when you can't control the outcome" (Restrepo 2019).

Brené Brown is known for her research on shame and vulnerability. My first experience with her work was when I watched her 2010 TED talk on vulnerability in 2019 (Brown 2010). The video had such a profound impact on me that I openly cried while riding on a train. A more current talk on this topic, including the quote above, is her Netflix special, *The Call to Courage* (Restrepo 2019).

My takeaway? Allow more vulnerability to exist in my life, in my relationships, in my work, with others, and with myself. The word authenticity also started to emerge in my vocabulary and my actions. *How could I walk the walk, and not just talk the talk?*

As I considered her thought process, I was brought back to earlier versions of myself. From a young age, I was labeled a crybaby by my mom. She did not like my tears and how easily they came. She wanted me to be strong. When I would show any sign of weakness or visibility of tears, she would call me "pissy-eyed." We spoke about this when I told her about my search for my biological family, and she gave me the history behind this "term of endearment."

She shared that I would always cry when she left the room, so she wanted me to toughen up and not be so soft. Hence, the name. She thought it would make me stop. It actually made it worse, but she did not know that.

I cry often, and quite easily. Tears are a way for me to release emotions and express myself. I do not see crying as a weakness. Quite the opposite; I see myself as brave for acknowledging and expressing my feelings. My tears flow in response to anger, sadness, frustration, disappointment, betrayal, and even joy. Sometimes I laugh until I cry.

I liked the idea of seeing myself as courageous. I loved the idea that vulnerability was a trait that could be admired, embraced, and revered. Brené Brown's definition of vulnerability validated my beliefs, which had previously been challenged throughout my life.

In her TED talk, she references the whole-hearted, and the attributes these types of individuals have in common. Their ability to be vulnerable and authentic is at the forefront of how they live their lives (Brown 2010).

At my core, I am expressive and a communicator. I've often wondered if these characteristics are natural tendencies I was born with. I was raised in an environment where true expression of emotions was not encouraged, and most often shut down or belittled, so I didn't learn them.

MY EXPRESSIVE NATURE WAS STIFLED
I did not have much practice exercising those muscles. In many relationships, both love and friendship, people told me I was imposing myself on them when I spoke the truth. When I shared an upset with a friend about how I felt I had been treated, often they turned it around on me.

The usual response was, "You are so sensitive. Why are you so needy?"

Typically, I accepted the feedback, assumed I was the issue, and buried what I had originally experienced. Since they disagreed with my assessment and dismissed what I felt, I took the blame. Ultimately, I apologized. I did not want to rock the boat or create a reason for them to leave.

I was compliant. I held back my emotions and told the teary-eyed, brokenhearted little girl inside of me to shut up. I reminded her what we had been taught, *"There's no room for your sadness. You can't let that hold you back. People won't accept or include your weepy ass or pissy eyes. You must be strong and self-sufficient. Needy and weak behavior will not be tolerated."*

As I got older, I became more intentional about when and if I held back my emotions. I still struggled with expressing negative emotions. If I thought I was left out or someone was pulling away, my neediness amplified. When my feelings weren't validated, I lashed out in anger.

If you knew me as a strong and resilient person, this tense and reactive version would be confusing. My outbursts blindsided others. Since I didn't understand how deep my insecurities and wounds ran, I didn't know how to temper my reactions. I appeared confident and at times assertive on the outside, yet I was a lonely little girl on the inside, deeply longing for acceptance and inclusion.

Recently someone described me as direct and matter-of-fact. I took exception to this description.

The person said, "Why do you think there is danger in being seen as direct?"

It was a reaction to how I perceived that part of me and the hurt I had caused with my sharp tongue in the past. I did not want to be portrayed or recognized in that way.

I have learned to re-parent that little girl who had not been able to work through her emotions. She was not given the space to experience or express what she felt. I have learned to manage and deal with my emotions better than before. When I feel like crying, I cry most times in the privacy and safety of my own home, though sometimes the tears will come in a mixed setting. When I get angry or frustrated, tears help me move through these feelings without overreacting.

Working in a very male-dominated industry, this one can get tricky. I have a colleague whom I trust implicitly. I've said to him, "There are going to be tears, so if you are uncomfortable with that, you may want to leave the room."

He has never left. I immensely value this about him.

When I need to address conflict, I do my best to find the right words and the right timing.

MINDFULNESS, PAUSING, AND REFLECTION ARE SUPER TOOLS

Ignoring past patterns can be challenging. I stay mindful and allow myself to process and reflect. Taking a pause before acting has been a powerful tool. For example, when my husband reminded me to take a breath before responding to my sister. That breath and pause can be the difference between a fair and equitable exchange of emotional information between two people versus an eruption where the other person feels attacked. In the latter scenario, the other person will be defensive, and nothing can be resolved in that energy.

When my sister rejected me on behalf of the entire family, I felt angry, upset, rejected, and betrayed—all the emotions that would trigger outbursts of anger in the past. That pause was critical. I was judging her, thinking she could have been more compassionate. However, by giving myself space to process, I thought about what this all might mean for her, her family, my mother, and other siblings. I had no idea what was going on in their lives or what they were contending with. Instead of imposing my expectation of compassion from her, I decided I would offer compassion, for them and myself.

My interpretation of being vulnerable means asserting myself peacefully without any attachment to the outcome. I know I am worthy of deep and meaningful connections, and I trust the right ones will always show up. We are conditioned to see ourselves through the lens of other people. We allow their reactions to define what we believe to be true about ourselves.

Even with the best intentions, people will impose their own stuff on you. Shame, guilt, fear, lack, scarcity mindset, control, codependency, anger, or whatever other unhealed aspects they may be carrying around could easily be transferred. We must each be responsible for holding our own stuff while engaging and living wholeheartedly.

I was aware risks existed. My greatest fear came true, they did not want to meet me. Thankfully, for the first time in my life, I felt equipped and ready for whatever the outcome, even this one. I called on my courage and allowed myself to be seen and vulnerable.

I was rejected by them, and that rejection hurt, but their response is not a reflection of me. They don't even know me. Her denial of my request and of my existence is about them. They may not have the capacity to handle whatever this means for them and whatever stories they have attached to the secret that I was born. I wish the outcome could have been different, but the timing is not right, yet again. While it hurts my heart not to be able to create any sort of communication with them right now and that I may miss the opportunity to meet my mother, I respect their decision. Everyone involved is an adult. We can all decide how we show up and what we do.

I remain willing and open to experience a connection if they ever change their minds. I have opened myself up to the joy of knowing whichever part of my family may come forth. I am immensely grateful for those who have already shown up for me. By being vulnerable and taking this risk, I have met amazing cousins and aunts who have made time and shown genuine interest in getting to know me.

I am proud of myself for being brave, stepping forward, and finding the missing parts of my story.

The story does not have a happy ending in the traditional sense, but I have closure with them for now.

CHAPTER 7

WHY NOW?

Timing is a critical component of my story and remains a point of contention as the adoption piece continued to unfold. When I attempted to contact my mother's family, their reaction challenged the timing of my outreach.

My biological sister and her husband both asked, "Why now? Why is she reaching out now, after all this time?"

At first, I was offended. How dare they question my timing or motives? I felt like they thought they had gotten away with the original abandonment. Since I had not contacted them after all these years, I must have no interest in finding them. They were in the clear. No one had to contend with the secret of my existence or deal with the burden of telling me why I was given up in the first place.

What they didn't realize was it took this long for me to be ready. Everyone had questions; theirs were reactive and defensive. When my adoptive mother originally broke the news to me, I also had questions, which were reactive and defensive.

Why did you wait so long to tell me? Why didn't my biological mother want me? Did I have more family? Why weren't they looking for me? Did they know I existed? Did my biological mother regret letting me go? Did my adoptive mother think she made a mistake by choosing me? And many, many more questions.

Each question came with a lesson and an opportunity: to learn more about myself; to heal my broken parts; and to discover the circumstances that brought me into this world. These details used to feel critically important, but I wonder what would truly change. At least now I know how my biological parents knew each other.

THE DETAILS IN OUR STORIES ARE PIVOTAL
When we think about our stories, most people can trace their beginnings back to pregnancy or, at a minimum, which hospital they were born.

For adoptees, it is different. Our stories generally start when we were adopted. Some families lovingly refer to that special time as "Gotcha Day," the date the child became part of their family.

I had neither beginning to my story until recently. Ironically, I didn't realize my adoptive mom and I never talked about her pregnancy or the day of my actual birth. I addressed this with my mom before she passed away. I asked her to tell me about the day she got me.

She shared, "You were about two weeks old, and we went to Jamaica Hospital with our lawyer. Your mother took you downstairs. She had to be there because she had to sign papers. Our friend AnnMarie—who you were named after—went and got you from your mother and brought you to us."

It was the first time I asked for details. My mom easily shared them, making me wonder why I had not asked before. I still don't know where I was for those first two weeks of my life. We assumed I stayed in the hospital, which means nurses took care of me, I suppose.

Thinking about childhood, I clearly remember the birth of my sister and brother. My sister was born when I was six, and my brother when I was nine. I was old enough to remember both pregnancies and births, so I had no reason to consider my mom didn't give birth to me. My adoptive mom and I often giggle about the fact I was not happy when she brought my sister home.

I told her, "I don't like it. Take it back."

As I reflect, I think it's odd I never asked about my birth. Perhaps because she was not with my father any longer, and I thought it would be painful for her. Once I found out I was adopted, I could not stop thinking about all the details that led to the day of my adoption. *How did my story begin? What did my biological mother feel when she found out she was pregnant? When did my adoptive mother learn about me? How did she feel when receiving the news about me?*

I asked my adoptive mom some of those questions. She had some answers but obviously not all of them.

As adoptees, it lends to a deeper meaning of how we end up where we do. I imagine many of the questions that have plagued me might also hold true for others whose birth and life stories have divided details. *What was my birth like? How did my story begin? How did I end up with my adoptive family?*

I do have some answers now, but it seems each time I fill in a missing detail, more questions emerge.

Once I learned about my adoption, I narrated a new story, which started like this: When I was twenty-five years old, I found out I was adopted. My mother didn't give me too many details at the onset. She shared that my biological mother lived in the same neighborhood as her during my early years.

She also told me, "Your biological mother had five kids, and when she got pregnant with you, she just couldn't afford to raise another child."

When I finally got my birth certificate, I learned she had three children when I was born, not the five I had been told. While that detail was corrected, that piece of paper did not provide any further insight regarding the decision to give me up.

Cue an influx of more questions, *Why was I the one she couldn't keep? Was she able to tell in the womb I would be a lot? Did she ever love me? Did she ever think about me? Did my siblings know I existed? Did they ever feel like something was missing, but they did not know why they felt that way?*

It was like reading a book, getting attached to a character, and finding out in the eighth Chapter that the character was completely different than how you understood them to be. Except the character was me, and this was my life. Things I understood to be true and foundations I had built my life on were shattered.

Betrayal can come in many shapes and sizes, and it feels, even as I put that word on the page here, like a strong reaction.

People react by speculating, "Your adoptive mother was just trying to protect you." "Your biological mother wanted you to have a better life than she could offer you."

These are likely accurate in some way. What was also true: I was a deep dark secret suppressed by my biological mother. How my life began was a secret in my adoptive family. Everyone who was part of my story, whether they were known or unknown to me, carried around secrets on my behalf. *Was I not to be trusted with the truth? Did they think I was not capable of handling it? Or were they so insecure in their own stories that they couldn't face their own truths?*

The question "Why now?" seems so simple and is a fair question. But it also suggests I don't have a right to know. *How dare she upset other people? How dare she reach out and try to find answers? Why can't she just be happy with how things are and leave well enough alone? Why does she think she has a right to disrupt our family?*

Another factor that always loomed when I thought about searching for my biological family was my adoptive mom's reaction. The concern that she would be hurt, or mad at me, was real. I was also worried she would think I didn't love her enough if I tried to find them. Compiled with the fears about abandonment and rejection I was already battling, the timing just never felt right.

MY ADOPTIVE MOTHER'S STORY AFFECTED MINE
I mentioned earlier that timing was a point of contention within my story. This was especially true when it came to my adoptive mother's decision to finally tell me the truth. I grappled with why she waited so long. I tried hard to see things from her perspective and considered she may have been wrestling with her own insecurities and fears. She was concerned about what me finding out would mean to our relationship. She had a hard life herself, and even so, she always did everything she could to make sure we were taken care of and provided for.

My mom was one of eleven children, and to say they had a rough childhood would be a grave understatement. I think she really wanted to have her own children so she could raise a family the way she wished she could have grown up. Things didn't quite work out the way she'd imagined.

My mom could be considered a controlling person, and our relationship and family dynamics were entrenched with deeply codependent behavior. I believe she felt she was protecting me. The challenge in that belief is I don't really know what she believes she was protecting me from. Her association with my adoption was rooted in scarcity.

She has shared with me, "I would see your biological mother in the neighborhood and would put a blanket over you. I even stopped going to the nearby gas station because sometimes she was there. I didn't want her to see you and try to take you back."

Her actions were governed by fear she might not be enough for me. I think she thought the way I felt about her might change if I knew I wasn't her biological daughter. I thought she might have been insecure about our connection and questioned whether our relationship would survive once I had the whole story. Perhaps she rationalized that by withholding this detail she ensured I would not feel like an outsider. In her mind, she removed the risk of me feeling left out or not fitting in with the family.

NO TRUE SENSE OF BELONGING
What's puzzling is I already felt like I didn't belong and couldn't identify what made me feel that way. I never necessarily felt or was treated differently than my brother or sister. I just had this odd feeling of not belonging. She didn't know this was going on with me. I kept it to myself. I had no reason to believe I was adopted. We had a family resemblance. One might not see an uncanny likeliness, but my siblings and I shared the same coloring and body proportions, though I was the shortest. None of us had the same biological father, so I attributed any physical differences to the paternal side of each of us.

I can't speculate how I would have acted had I known the truth earlier. It would be unfair and untruthful to claim that had I known as a child or teenager, my feelings and experiences would have been altered.

When I was in the fifth grade, John and my mom sat me down and explained to me that he wanted to adopt me. John told me the decision was totally my choice, and no matter what I decided, it wouldn't change how he felt about me. This was a big decision to impose on a ten-year-old.

I assessed the offer. I thought about the way we were seated alphabetically at school, and I liked where my seat was in the classroom. Since John's last name started with a G, and mine with an S, accepting meant I would change my name and ultimately my seat. I declined the offer for him to adopt me, as I didn't want to move seats in class. That represented the depth of my decision-making skills at that age.

Are you wondering why they didn't tell me I was adopted at that time? It seemed like the perfect opportunity. That has popped into my head multiple times. If I had that knowledge then, I may have gone in a different direction. Of course, I can't say for sure. I *can* say my decision was based on what I believed to be true at the time.

When I was reeling from the news that day in St. Augustine and started to process, this memory popped up. I thought, "That would have a been another perfect opportunity to tell me." Like the thoughts about knowing my cousins were adopted, or when they decided to send me to Arizona.

I also started blaming myself. *How could you miss this? Does everyone except me know about this? How come you didn't pay closer attention to the specifics?*

TIME TO FLIP THE SCRIPT

I had been in therapy before moving to Florida. I was in my early twenties, and I just couldn't get a handle on my anger. I thought therapy would help. Finding the right therapist took a few attempts, but eventually I found one and stayed with her for a while. This was before learning about my adoption. Reviewing the timing of this, and the events that shaped the next thirty years of my life, more therapy would have been beneficial. I have not done that yet but do not rule it out for the future.

I went in another direction, which was also helpful. In 2013 I hired my first coach. Initially it was because I wanted to sell my business, and I knew I would benefit from some guidance. Finding the right match also took a little figuring out, just as it had with finding the right therapist. I ended up working with Lara. She focused on energy healing, specifically within your body.

During my work with her, a lot came up about my birth family and the family who raised me. Years of patterns, beliefs, behaviors, and emotions I had never properly learned how to express or manage. Not only had I not properly handled them, but also the energy of all the unexpressed emotions remained stuck and stagnant in my body.

Through that work, I learned many things about myself, including how much power I had given to others and how I allowed them to treat me. Of course, how others treat me impacts me, but ultimately, I don't need the validation and acceptance of others to feel complete or worthy. This was a huge lesson in my life, and one I continually revisit. It's like a muscle you need to work on constantly to strengthen and build.

When my biological sister denied my request to connect, I came back to this lesson. I felt sadness, rejection, and abandonment, but instead of being devastated, I was able to attach a new story to it. I did not allow her response to affect how I saw myself or become a reflection of my worthiness.

I am still the same person I was before her rejection. Nothing material changed, and my life remains unaffected by their lack of acceptance or inclusion. I was disappointed they didn't want to meet me or take any time to get to know me. However, what was most noticeable was her lack of compassion and curiosity. She came across as a victim, as if I did something to her and her family.

Through this practice of working with a coach, I became more open to my own possibilities and started to have a more abundant approach to life. Hard things still happened, and conflict still occurred. I still experienced moments of feeling let down or misunderstood. However, my ability to cope and process elevated as a result of the work I was doing.

When I turned fifty, I was reminded that time is finite. From that moment on, I knew I needed to be more discerning about how I spent my time and expended my energy. I continued to invest in myself and worked with coaches, teachers, mentors, and guides. I still do. I was not alone. I am not alone.

Another powerful lesson I uncovered was when you blame somebody you give away all your power. By blaming my adoptive mom for not telling me sooner, I was giving away my power. If her objective was truly to protect and not to control me, I could look at her situation through a lens of love. I recognized and felt how much she loved me and how painful it must have been for her not to feel confident enough in our relationship to trust me with the truth. She wasn't wrong; we had a tumultuous life for quite some time. We experienced disruption often. She didn't want to add to that by telling me I was adopted.

I've done a lot of forgiving and letting go, which is necessary under these circumstances. This created tremendous space to be open to new experiences and stories and allowed me to see all the events from a different vantage point. I understand everyone is doing the best they can.

I am grateful to my mom for choosing me and for always fighting to have me in her life. I accept the story for how it's played out and have let go of any resentment I felt for not being trusted to handle the truth earlier.

I choose to believe my biological mother did what she felt was the best thing she could for me as well.

Timing has played a huge role in this story. A part remains unwritten, and I need to have patience. I recognize others need time too. If my siblings did not know about me, they would have much to understand and hopefully work through as a family. I do hope I get an opportunity to meet my biological mother and hear the story from her directly.

I will hold on to that hope and remember how long it took my adoptive mom to tell me, and then how long it took me to get the courage to look for them. The only problem is I don't think we can afford another twenty-five or thirty years, so hopefully something will happen sooner. If it doesn't, I will move forward and be grateful for what I do know and all the blessings I have experienced in my life so far. I may try to contact other family members at some point. I have not made any final decisions regarding that. In this moment, I don't feel the urgency to continue to chase them to meet me.

This support system I have cultivated is the ultimate answer to my biological sister and her husband's question, "Why now?"

Why now, big sis? Because the timing was right for me. I am secure with where I am in life. I have tools to support me when I get rejected for a second time by the same people. I have a beautiful, loving, and supportive group of friends and family guiding me through this process. I have the capacity to recognize your reaction to my existence doesn't define who I get to be in this world or how I tell my story.

Even though my biological mother and sister are not ready to talk to or meet me, I do not have any regrets about pursuing my search for the missing piece of my story. I am not a secret,

I am not a mistake, I am not a burden, and I am certainly not ashamed I exist!

We are all adults, and we can all decide how we choose to handle the facts.

I choose to have gratitude for my life. I am grateful my biological mother gave me life. I accept she was not intended to raise me, and my adoptive mother was meant to take that role. I am grateful my mother chose to adopt me and did her best to protect me.

I have no guilt for having questions and for asking them.

Why now? Because it is my life, and therefore my timing.

I am ready!

CHAPTER 8

MY THREE DADS

My earliest childhood memories start around the age of five. One unhappy memory is still quite vivid and involved my mother's husband at the time. We lived in a one-bedroom apartment, and my bed was the sofa. He came home drunk and assumed I was asleep. I was not but pretended to be. He got physical with my mother. I was afraid he would hurt her, me, or both of us. She stood up to him, especially to protect me. This particular memory brings me back to the first time I felt unsafe. I learned at a tender age not all men, nor all relationships, were built the same. Safety became a theme in my life with layers that continued to unfold.

My adoptive father was her first husband. Then the guy described above, and then John.

By the time my adoptive mom was thirty-five, she had been married four times, twice to the same man. She had three children, two biologicals from two different men, and one adopted.

She divorced the guy who was abusive. She had not had any children with him, thankfully. Next my sister's biological father came into the picture. They did not marry, but he was active in my sister's life for a while. After they split, he would still pick up my sister, and he would always take me too. He made me feel included, and I remember looking forward to those visits. And it made me wonder why my own father didn't take that type of interest.

When she married John, it felt like we could finally settle into a more traditional family story. His stability was good for us, especially for me. I craved that in my life, and he brought it. He and my mom had their struggles through the years, but he was always there, despite what was going on with them.

My youngest brother is John's biological son, but he never made my sister or me feel less than. As far as he was concerned, we were all his kids. He was fair, engaged, and showed a genuine interest in our well-being. That was new to me. John was the first time I experienced what it was like to have a dad.

MY BIOLOGICAL DAD
When I learned about my biological father, I experienced a different type of knowing and connection to someone, unlike anything I had known prior. His was named William, but they referred to him as Billy. The initial photos I received were mainly of him as a boy. My aunt generously went through her photos and shared more of him when he was about twenty years old. At that time, I was already born, though he likely had no idea about me.

I won't say it was like looking in a mirror, but I did see myself reflected through the photos, especially in his facial expressions. One thing I do not have is a poker face. You can always tell what's going on with me just by looking at me. I saw that similarity in those photos of Billy.

He died when he was twenty-one years old, and I was just two. In one of the pictures, he was holding my cousin who was born a month before me. That could have very well been me instead if he had only known. I felt incredibly sad he was denied that opportunity. I don't know how that would have changed anything for him, but it felt unfinished.

He didn't get to know a part of him existed in this world, a baby girl. A deep longing to talk to him emerged too. If only I could have a conversation with him, hear his voice.

My cousins have described him based on what they remember. They said he was a protector of his sisters. He seemed to be a caretaker from a young age. My aunt and I have talked a little about him and how he grew up fast. My grandfather died when my father was sixteen years old, and he became the man of the house. He worked and helped my grandmother take care of the family.

I like to speculate that spending time with my biological mother was a respite for him. It might have even been for her as well. Perhaps they found some modicum of escape with each other.

I never met this man, and he did not know I existed, yet I feel an accessibility to him. Our souls know each other.

I was taken aback by the depth of grief I experienced when I learned his life ended tragically and suddenly. I wonder if he would have understood me.

MY ADOPTIVE DAD
In September 2020, my adoptive father passed away. I had not seen him since I was fourteen years old, in Arizona that summer before high school. I am Facebook friends with his biological daughter. She and I were not close, but I was aware of her strong relationship with him. Sometimes I looked at their photos and wondered what it would have been like if he had raised me. I am aware social media does not always depict reality, but from my brief interactions with her, it seemed she truly cared for him. He was very present and engaged in her life, completely opposite to his absence in mine.

When I learned of his passing, I reached out to her to offer my condolences.

She replied to me, "Oh my gosh, I was going to reach out to you. We were cleaning out my dad's personal belongings, and I found photos and a letter in his jewelry box that I thought you might want."

Learning he had kept them for over forty years blew me away. It was so generous of her to make time to tell me and send them to me, especially during a time when she was in mourning. I waited in anticipation for the package to arrive. I was incredibly curious which pictures they were, and specifically wondered about the letter since I didn't have any recollection of interacting with him.

When the package finally arrived, I found the following photos: three-year-old me with Santa; five-year-old me; seven-year-old me; and fourteen-year-old me, and a letter dated March 24, 1981, about five months before I went to visit him in August that year.

The letter was simple and read, "Dear Dad, here are the most recent pictures I have. They were just taken for our yearbook for graduation. The only thing that is different is I got new glasses and my hair is longer. Write back soon. Love ya, AnnMarie."

Apparently how I avoided saying I love you was by saying "love ya."

By the way, I don't think he ever wrote me, so I think it's interesting I wrote "Write back soon."

Emotion flooded through me as I examined the faces in the pictures. My mom didn't have many pictures of me from my childhood and definitely not at those ages. The five-year-old and seven-year-old photos bore the most resemblance to my biological dad. I experienced a deep gratitude that my adoptive father kept these memories of me.

It felt like such a gift, and for the first time ever I felt a connection to this man, though he was now passed. Odd for that to take place twice, both after they were gone. This newly formed heart bond with a man I barely knew, yet I carry his name, as well as an even more recent soul bond for a man I never met, but I carry his DNA, added some completion to my fragmented life story.

I deeply appreciated that his daughter did not throw away the photos. She took the time to contact me and send them to me. I felt comradery with her, and I was very grateful for her openness with me. We had been chatting on Messenger, and I finally summoned the courage to ask her if she knew I was adopted.

I assumed she figured it strange I was not mourning "our" dad.

Her answer, "My brother and I knew you were adopted when you came to visit, but we were sworn to secrecy."

More people in on the secret. More layers of betrayal surrounded my story. I don't blame her at all. They were just kids. We were all kids, but what a mess!

During that exchange, she sent me this message, "I am sorry you never got to know the Dad I knew. He was truly a fantastic father, and I've always struggled with why the father I knew didn't have a relationship with his first daughter."

Hearing that made me feel hollow and like an outsider, again. I know her intention was not to make me feel that way, but I couldn't avoid it. It was demonstrative of how disengaged I was from the people who were supposed to be my core.

I wrote back to her. "Honestly, I don't think it was all him. It's complicated. I always intended to try and have a relationship with him once I was older, but when I found out I was adopted I assumed he didn't want me. I am not bitter at all.

Just disappointed there were so many lies. I know it was my mom's choice not to tell me."

This was cathartic for me, and receiving the photos bridged something. Perhaps I made some sort of impact on his life. He held on to them for all these years. That felt meaningful for me and created a shift in how I thought he had felt about me.

A SAFE PLACE TO EXPRESS
A couple of years ago I created a private Facebook group. As I considered transitioning to a career in coaching, I wanted to have a safe place where I and my members could be vulnerable. At that point in time, I was not comfortable sharing deeply personal details on my public Facebook page. That summer I had grown the group to almost three hundred members.

When I received the package, I wanted to talk to someone about it and took the conversation to that Facebook group. I created a post and wrote about the choices that were made and how they affected many aspects of my life. I shared my background story about fear of abandonment and lack of self-esteem—my thoughts of *Why would anyone choose me?* I revealed the truth about my growth and healing, and the incidents that led me there.

In this specific post I talked about some recent inner child work I had done, connecting back to seven-year-old me, and how ironic it was that one of the photos was of seven-year-old me. I could now see the face of this child I was comforting and helping heal her old wounds. That was a huge breakthrough for me. I had previously resisted inner child work, citing I didn't really "get it."

A direct quote from that share: "The layers of our lives are verses in our story or chapters in our book" (October 15, 2020).

When I wrote that post, I had no idea I would be writing a book about my adoption journey. This newly discovered data that my adoptive father didn't fully abandon me gave me hope and strength. The fact he kept something to remind him of me for forty years allowed me to rewrite the conspiracy story I had committed to.

MY STEPDAD CHANGED MY LIFE
Thinking about how each of these men influenced my life in some way, the strongest and most consistent influence was John. His presence in my life was a critical turning point for me. I always felt seen by him. He was not an emotionally expressive man, but you always knew where you stood with him. I knew he was proud of me.

One time my parents came back to New York City for a visit. I planned a special vacation for them. We visited Atlantic City, stayed in Manhattan, and spent time on Long Island with family. Even though they had both lived in New York their entire lives before Florida, they rarely did anything special. They were always working and trying to make ends meet. I wanted them to experience NYC the way I had come to love it. The trip was amazing and very special.

One night we were out for dinner at a restaurant downtown at the South Street Seaport, with a view of the Brooklyn Bridge. We ordered a dessert that was a replica of the bridge, and when it came, John looked at me.

He shook his head and said, "This girl. She really is something else."

For him, that was a deep compliment. A few words from him went a very long way.

I did my best to help him understand that he gave me the confidence to push outside of my comfort zone. I wanted him to know I felt more secure and capable once he showed up in my life. He had a way of running interference with my mom and me, which was needed on a regular basis. He was the one who was protecting me.

Two of my most meaningful memories from the day I got married were him walking me down the aisle and our father-daughter dance. A funny instance happened when we were supposed to walk down the aisle. The wedding planner had given Anderson's cousins the job of unrolling the "white carpet," a runner that covered the middle section which I would walk down. They were having trouble unrolling it and got stuck halfway down the aisle. My dad and I were waiting for them to be done, which did not seem like it was going to happen.

Music was a big part of our wedding preparation, and when we got to the point of the song where I was supposed to be walking down the aisle, I said to my dad, "Okay, we need to go now."

He responded, "We can't. They are not done."

To which I responded, "Nope, watch this." I looked at the cousins and said, "Guys, that's enough. We need to get moving."

We promptly stepped over the carpet roll and walked toward the front where Anderson was waiting. My dad had an incredible ability to show up in the capacity in which I needed him. This was a great example. He just went with what I asked of him. No resistance.

When planning the father-daughter dance, I was very intentional about finding a song that accurately represented my bond to him.

I chose "Music of My Heart" by NSYNC and Gloria Estefan. The lyrics truly personified what I felt for him and what he meant in my life. He saved me. He was the first person to truly let me be myself. He encouraged it! With him in my corner, I felt I could soar. The limits and fears I had felt in the past had lessened. Having him as my father from the age of eight truly helped to free the me inside.

I wanted him to know how much he meant to me and how much his presence in my life made a huge difference for me. He taught me work ethics, strong family values, moral decision-making, and so much more. He was the smartest person I've ever known, and he was always reading and learning.

He passed In December 2012, and I was devastated when I got the call from my mom. His passing was sudden and unexpected. We didn't talk often, but I always felt him. When I was truly stuck, I knew he would help me figure it out. I miss him deeply, and I could have really used his support over this past year.

Someone asked me recently if I was angry toward him for holding the secret of my adoption. Until now, I had not thought about that. I don't remember how I felt toward him when I learned the news. I guess because he was not married to my mom when I was adopted, I didn't hold him responsible. Plus, I know no one could make my mom do something she was not ready to do, not even him.

He always made me feel like I had place in the family and that I had a home, no matter what. I could not find any reason to be upset with him when all that unfolded. He has been gone for more than ten years now, but he will always remain the music of my heart. I did not carry his name or his DNA, but I carried his heart. He was my father, and he was my dad.

IT'S COMPLICATED
It feels complicated to have three dads, yet to only know one of them, and for them all to be gone now.

Each one had an influence on me. My interpretation of what I meant to them shaped my own relationships. What I understood to be true about how they felt about me affected my own beliefs and my ability to believe I was worthy.

I chose to marry a man who was a lot like John. Anderson is stable, consistent, and always concerned about my safety.

As I continue to work on my own growth and healing, I have gained a deeper understanding of the men who have influenced me and impacted my life.

I realize I've told myself stories about why I wasn't wanted. I recognize the circumstances were far more convoluted than I could understand at ages five, eight, fourteen, and throughout my life. I released the self-imposed burden of being convinced I wasn't enough and wasn't wanted.

Many circumstances affected why things played out the way they did.

I graciously embrace what each of these men meant to me, and what I meant to them.

CHAPTER 9

HOW OTHERS SEE US VERSUS HOW WE SEE OURSELVES

OPINIONS OF OTHERS LEAVE LASTING EFFECTS
When I shared the post in my Facebook group (Santamarina-Hidalgo 2020) about the photos from my adoptive dad, I received an overwhelming response of support and gratitude, which was comforting. To provide a little background on the membership of the group, I personally know almost everyone, some for a very long time and some I had met more recently. What shocked me was how quickly the responses rolled in and the type of feedback they offered.

One friend wrote (October 15, 2020), "AnnMarie, thank you for sharing your story. In high school I was in awe of you. You always had a smile on your beautiful face, and you were always so happy."

To which another friend commented (October 15, 2020), "AnnMarie and I were in the same friend group in junior high school. We were a tight group that was trying to navigate the teenage years. I too admired AnnMarie's confidence and intelligence."

That tight group she referenced was the group who dumped me before high school. She went to a different school and was not part of that real-life mean girl episode. Ironically, she admired my strength and confidence, yet our mutual friends did not deem me worthy to continue our friendship.

Regarding that group from my Arizona teenage abandonment episode, one of them reached out to me in the early days of Facebook and sent me a friend request. I was instantaneously transported back to 1981. I reluctantly accepted the invitation.

She sent me a private message in September 2008, which said, "We were really mean to you back in school, but it seems to me your life has turned out really well, so shame on us."

She apologized for the incident and caught me up on her life. I appreciated her acknowledgment of the situation. That was an early moment when I noticed everyone is dealing with their own stuff. You never know what someone else is going through. The more connected you are to yourself, the better you can navigate when other people are inflicting their wounded selves on you.

We were kids, and that was a long time ago. We came to the point a while later that we decided to plan a small reunion with the entire group. As we were making plans to meet up, the anticipation filled me with anxiety. *What if this was just a ploy to leave me out again? Why would they want to hang out with me now?* The awkward, lonely fourteen-year-old thought this was a bad idea. Adult AnnMarie decided it was safe, and it turned out to be just fine. We had a really nice time, and it gave me closure on an old story I had been carrying around like a tattered blanket.

Facing our fears can be painful and scary, and most of the time we avoid it. I am proud of myself for showing up. I was able to create a new story. We are not best friends, and we only saw each other once, but we are friendly and that past is behind me. I am good friends with the mutual friend who was not part of their rejecting me, and she is so generous with her feedback and support. I am very grateful to her.

Reverting to the comments from the Facebook group, I had a hard time reconciling the way they saw me. They described me as confident, beautiful, intelligent, and happy. If you asked me to outline how I saw myself as a teenager, I would tell you I was insecure, awkward, longing to be included, and dying to find a place I truly belonged. I had no idea they saw me the way they did, neither then nor now.

The other part I was a bit taken aback by was their willingness to post their comments to a group of three hundred people, almost forty years later. My heart was beyond full. The validation I had been seeking my whole life showed up but in an unexpected and incredibly beautiful way. I did not share that post seeking anything. I created it because I thought it might resonate with others who could be holding on to old stories, thereby blocking love and abundance.

This whole exchange led me to think about how others see me and how I see myself.

SEEKING VALIDATION CAN FEEL LIKE AN ANCHOR
Through the pages of this book, I've shared that I've felt, experienced, and demonstrated anger, hurt, betrayal, being left out, and abandonment. At this point in my journey, I have other words to describe myself and how I strive to show up in the world.

I am compassionate, resilient, abundant, articulate, playful, generous, and an incredibly loving person. I still feel hurt at times or get angry at situations. Sometimes people, but mostly situations cause me to feel nervous and scared or unsure of myself. These are feelings I've had but not necessarily words that describe me. Learning the distinction between who I am, what I do, and how I react to things has provided me with a powerful reframe of the stories I tell myself and the beliefs I carry focused on what others think about me.

A college friend commented on my post (October 15, 2020) that she worked at an adoption agency for five years and she offered the ultimate validation. "You are not alone," she wrote. "It was very common for people not to tell their kids they were adopted. Especially in the forties, fifties, sixties, and seventies. I remember reading some women would stuff their stomachs to look pregnant to pass a child as their own."

She shared her opinion that she always felt biological families who gave up their children were selfless. As I had learned through the continued stories from other adoptees, the feelings carried around about adoption were common. The people in my life who were telling me I was broken had not been through the same experience I had. They could not know how I felt. To fully understand the plight of the adopted gave me the permission I needed to break from the binds that tied me to negative versions of myself.

I reveled in the positive feedback and received the words with an open heart and mind.

A friend I met through my coaching class and spent many hours getting to know on Zoom also commented on October 15, 2020, "This is one of the bravest, most beautiful pieces of personal reflection I've ever read. It is my privilege to be your friend."

This comment stood out to me. *A privilege to be my friend? Could I believe that sentiment? Would that make me selfish or too big for my britches? Or would it just make me gracious to be able to accept the opinion of someone who is my friend and shared generously what my post meant to him?*

My friend Nicole has always supported me, and her comment reminded me she was by my side, (October 15, 2020), "Keep up the good work, girl. And like I told you yesterday, I'm your girl. As a fellow adoptee, I know exactly what you're feeling. One of the happiest days of my life was meeting my biological family, especially my three brothers. Keep on going, and I'm here to help, catch, guide, and lean on if you need me."

My friendship with Nicole had already spanned forty-five years, and she was still there for me. That does not mean all those years were perfect. I've disappointed her, and we had some disagreements along the way.

One time she told me, "I keep trying to be your close friend, and you keep pushing back. I don't get it."

That was an eye-opener for me because I was not intentionally behaving that way, but she was right. I put up walls. I was very grateful to her for being so open with me. It made our friendship stronger, and I became aware she valued time with me. It was not always easy for me to believe that. Her determination to maintain our friendship reinforced a new belief. When people get to know the real me, they stick around and fight for the friendship because I am worth it.

CONNECTION IS AN INSIDE JOB
In her book *The Gifts of Imperfection*, Brené Brown writes, "I define connection as the energy that exists between people when they feel seen, heard, and valued; when they can give and receive without judgment; and when they derive sustenance and strength from the relationship" (Brown 2022).

What I experienced through the outpouring of support, reflection, and reciprocated vulnerability, touched and inspired me. As I wrote this Chapter and shared this story, I revisited the honest exchange with these people I trusted, and I realized I had successfully rewritten my abandonment story.

It started with a simple invite to a private Facebook group. I invited people I trusted to see this deeper, personal version of me, even if it was on social media. I counted on their acceptance, and they delivered, authentically and courageously.

All the participants engaged from a place of positivity and connection. I had desired this type of belonging my entire life, and it felt even more reassuring as I realized I had attracted this! I was the common thread in the group. People knew me, and when I asked them to join, they said yes! And they kept showing up for me, for others, and for themselves.

This entire revelation felt as if I had pulled back dark drapes that had been covering the windows for such a long time, and a rich blue sky with magnificent rays of sunshine beaming down was waiting on the other side. The lesson? Don't be afraid to let the light in.

Connection can feel like a far-reaching goal when you don't acknowledge it starts with you. Inner connection is the foundation on which the rest is built and cultivated.

This new lesson started to emerge and unfold for me. I've always considered myself an outgoing person, and for the most part, people are drawn to me. That feels uncomfortable saying out loud, but it's a truth. I am not shy about having a conversation with someone I don't know. And I do my best to be present and engaged. I have received feedback that I have a natural way of making people feel comfortable.

I am curious by nature and ask people questions with genuine interest to learn more about them. Sometimes I ask too many questions! I can get lost in the details. Regardless, these attributes help foster genuine connection.

The contradiction was that voice in my head challenging me, *Don't get too attached. They are going to leave once they know you.* I blocked truly meaningful connections to protect myself.

As I thought about friendships that had waned through the years, I was usually the one to back off or lose interest. If I thought someone was getting too close, or if I was feeling too dependent on their presence in my life, I shut down or backed away, for fear they would leave me. I left first to maintain the upper hand.

My view on connection is that it is a mutual understanding and an ease of communication, even with difficult conversations. This is in alignment with Brené Brown's definition. I spent a lot of time striving to cultivate external connections and didn't realize I wasn't being true to my own identity. I allowed others to define me and believed things they told me about myself, especially the negative and degrading things. This started with my parents, then teachers, friends, boyfriends, bosses, coworkers, and sometimes people who didn't have any direct value in my life.

I was not taught how to cultivate a strong sense of self and was discouraged from prioritizing myself, ultimately creating a grave dependency on validation from others. Manifesting authentic connection with others was hard when I was so disconnected from myself. This was another huge breakthrough.

When my business partner and I started our company, he would often say to me, "Why do you need people to tell you that you did a good job? If you know you did well, that should be enough."

I thought he was being difficult and withholding praise. However, for him, it was simply that when he knew he did a good job, he did not need someone else to tell him. That was unfamiliar to me. Even though I've grown a lot, I still crave validation and acceptance from certain authority figures. I remain a work in progress and am committed to keep doing the work.

HIGHER SELF AND EGO ARE IN BATTLE
As I embarked on my journey of healing and growing, I learned about the "higher self." If this term is not familiar or self-explanatory, "higher self" implies a spiritual connotation to a higher, more evolved self that encourages us to step out of our battered, and often limited, "human" version. By expanding our lens, we can greatly increase the scope of what's possible for us.

That term felt abstract to me, and initially it felt like something made-up. However, as the work progressed, I found myself leveling up, rising, and becoming a more evolved and understood version of myself. The concept of higher self became more of a goal and less of a made-up construct.

This also brought me back to that selfish version that was described and mirrored to me as a kid. I was learning how to stand up for what I wanted and express my needs, but that behavior was greeted with retaliation, and I was told I was selfish. My expanded awareness now knows those were limitations imposed on me by others who were swirling in their own fears and insecurities.

Higher self and ego can oftentimes conflict with each other. Ego defined in simple terms is the way a person perceives themselves, how an individual thinks, feels, and distinguishes themselves from the rest. Ego is a person's sense of self-esteem or self-importance. Although the word ego often carries a negative connotation—as in egocentric or egotistical—in actuality, the ego has both positive and negative aspects. From the positive perspective, ego simply means a solid, healthy, and strong sense of self, which by now we know I did not have.

When I prioritize or express my needs, my ego transports to the young "selfish" child I was forced to believe I was. My mind focuses on what I've been taught: Asking for what you need or want is bad. *"How dare you ask for that? Who do you think you are?"*

When those thoughts proliferate my intention, I pause and check in. *Am I coming from a place of love? Am I digging my heels in and being a spoiled brat?* If I know I am letting my heart lead the way, I trust that protecting what I need is not selfish. It is self-care.

One of my coaching teachers suggested we give our ego a name, personify it, so when it appears, we can face it head on. I call mine Edith. She is not all bad. Edith can keep me grounded. She reminds me to connect to past experiences to ensure I am not acting on a feeling or whim or reacting to something that has hurt or traumatized me in the past. Our ego protects us too. It takes a keen sense of self-awareness to be able to discern when we are being limited or looked out for.

Have you ever heard "rejection is protection"? This is a great example of using the ego for a higher purpose. When you are being rejected in some way, this can feel like the end of world. If you didn't get a job you wanted, or a deal fell through, or a home you had your heart set on went to a higher bidder, maybe that is because something in one of those scenarios would have been detrimental down the road. By having it taken away, there is room for something new, and potentially a whole lot better.

Edith can also be the loudest and sometimes meanest voice in my head. She represents a compilation of memories where people did not show up, or left, or didn't choose me. When she is afraid I might be heading down a path where I could be in danger again, she incites all the reasons why an idea won't work or a person I may want to know has no interest in knowing me. My responsibility is to parse these thoughts and determine what's real and what's defensive of old stories.

Things Edith says to me: *"Why would people want to read your book? Who cares what you have to say? Why would people join your community? Who would hire you for a coach? Why do you think you are qualified to help other people in their lives?"*

These are built on versions of real-life interactions I've experienced. "You think you are too big for your britches." "Oh, who's better than you?" "My daughter, everything with her is a business transaction." "Why are you so needy? I don't know that part of you, and when she comes out, I don't like her; it makes me uncomfortable." "You've checked out."

The real-life versions are all things people in my life have said to me. There is more, but you get the point. I don't deny the statements may warrant some relevance. My behavior at a given time provoked someone to say these things to me, but they are not who I am.

The distinction between who I am and what I do is still unraveling in my life. I have gained a new perspective, so growth has absolutely occurred. Now when someone tells me they see me and suggests I am confident, beautiful, or smart, I say, "Thank you."

Conversely, if someone makes a snide comment in observation of my life, I likely also will say, "Thank you."

Old patterns would find me defending or explaining myself. I try not to do that anymore.

I am not perfect, and I've exuded less-than-perfect behaviors throughout my lifetime. When my less than generous self shows up and wants to disrupt things, I examine inward and try to better understand what's driving my behavior. *Why don't I have any compassion? Am I being judgmental of myself or others? Why am I allowing this person to say disparaging things about me? What can I do to be my higher self in this situation? I am worthy.*

I am truly enjoying the gift of knowing and understanding myself better.

EVERYONE IS DOING THE BEST THEY CAN

Another lesson Lara taught me was everyone is doing the best they can in any given moment. When I find myself in conflict with someone, I aim to remember they are wrestling with their own issues.

For instance, when my biological sister told me her family had no interest in speaking with me, she also said "at this time."

Perhaps that was intentional on her part, or just what she wrote. By stepping back from what I wanted, I recognized they may have had stuff happening in their own family that did not give them room to tackle the fact they had another sibling. I still don't know if they didn't know I existed, and therefore needed time to process. I still don't know if they will ever change their minds, but I am not building a story around their rejection to say I am unworthy of their love or connection. I continue to remind myself it has nothing to do with me. They don't know me; therefore, they are rejecting the *idea of me, not me as a person.*

Previous versions of myself would have stopped at, "I am not good enough, and that's why they don't want me." But I know I bring plenty into the relationship were they ever to reconsider. With the right timing, we might get to know each other.

One of my greatest lessons is the recognition that when I bring my true and whole self into a conversation or interaction, magic happens. As I get more refined in my values and what makes me tick, I've learned to respectfully put boundaries in place. I recognized I don't need to give away all of myself for people to accept and love me.

This statement seems as if ego is in charge and I don't care about others. But my experience has been the contrary. The more secure and connected to myself I am, the more capacity I have available to give to others. I love creating, cultivating, and participating in meaningful conversations. The topics vary in scope and depth and cover many areas, such as my dreams, other's dreams, struggles, complications, challenges, lessons, and reflections.

This list is long. The common denominators are truth, vulnerability, and a space of nonjudgment. In these interactions the participants are present and engaged with each other. That feels like bliss to me.

I do still have people in my life who are not the wholehearted, like Brené Brown describes. Those people don't always have the capacity to demonstrate grace and compassion. I may find myself being blamed for something I was not responsible for or being shunned by someone who believes I did not nurture our friendship the way they expected me to.

If they did not get what they needed from me, and I was doing the best I could with what I had available to me and it still wasn't enough, then that friendship dissolved or that client chose another option.

When those things happen, it does not mean I am loser or a failure. It represented a specific letdown or falling short in those moments. I didn't have the capacity at that time to give any more than I had given. It could also be the friendship or the job opportunity was just not in alignment with my highest self. I trust that now.

Not everything is right for us. We can't be everything to everyone.

I crave more ease in my life. If I am fighting for something that doesn't seem to want to be with me, or for me, that is a good indication to let go or move on. I am not making excuses, but I am also not carrying around everyone else's opinions of me.

FEEDBACK IS ASKED FOR AND OPINIONS ARE NOT

In an article published by Myriam Hadnes, she shares:

Among all benefits of asking for feedback, the most prominent is the one that allows us to prepare our own mindset for an eventual setback. In fact, evidence shows that we are more open to critical comments when we feel safe, trust, and have gratitude because we sense the good intention of our counterpart. The obstacle, though, is that we feel trust toward those who are similar to us but learn most from those who are not because they show us what we don't see and teach us what we don't know (Hadnes 2018).

That concept of being more open to feedback when we feel safe continues to play out in my story. I invite you to think about how this works in your own life. Consider how people offer you feedback. Is it coming from a place of safety and from a trusted individual? Or is it being imposed on you by those not looking closely at themselves?

In that article, Myriam notes, "We tend to forget that feedback addresses our behavior and not our identity, and thereby ignore that it might be appropriate, objective, or helpful" (Hadnes 2018).

I encourage you to pay closer attention to whose voice is the loudest in your head. How much of your identity is determined by you versus others you've given this power to? Recognize your Edith. What will you call yours? Learn to communicate on a deeper level.

The more in tune you are with who you are taking direction from, the more you can take back your power, where you may have given it away.

Think about your higher self. When does it show up? How is your higher self contributing to your decision-making? Listen closely to the conversations you are having with others and with yourself. The ability to recognize how you speak to yourself and how you allow others to speak to you could change your life.

CHAPTER 10

CAN I OWN MY TRUTH WITHOUT HURTING OTHERS?

I carried the burden of guilt and concern about how others will react to my actions for most of my life. *How would my adoptive mom feel about my search and my findings? How would both my biological and adoptive families feel about the fact I am publicly sharing my story?*

I've come to a crossroad where I can no longer hold myself back out of fear. It is not my intention to hurt anyone in this process. If I can't be true to myself, I end up the one who gets hurt.

When I first met Pamela Slaton and decided to work with her, I became aware of her book, *Reunited* (Slaton 2012).

A wonderful read, it reinforced many of the beliefs I've held on to. Through her words she legitimized so many of the notions I had been grappling with. She openly recognized that as adoptees we can't escape the desire to know. Even when we have wonderful, loving parents and nurturing tight-knit families, that need to know is always lurking (Slaton 2012).

She has worked with over three thousand clients searching for someone—a parent searching for a child, a child searching for a parent, siblings searching for each other, and many other variations. In the introduction of her book, she talks about both her clients and her own experience since she is also adopted.

I was always concerned my adoptive mother would feel like I was trying to replace her.

Pam speaks about precisely those wants I denied and avoided for so long:

"It's not a matter of replacing an existing family. They don't expect to find some love they never had. It's not some selfish quest for more affection. It's about acknowledgment. It's about being able to say to your birth mother, *I'm okay. I had a good life. You did the right thing. I hope you moved on with your life. I hope you're okay, too.* Searching for one's origins means nothing less than validating one's existence" (Slaton 2012).

Acknowledgment and validation are words that jumped off the page into my own heart. Yes! Thank you for spelling out what it feels like to be in this position.

She also says, "I don't care how old you are. When you are an adopted child, the desire to know can last a lifetime. And when you are a birth parent, that knowledge is always with you. You never forget" (Slaton 2012).

As much as her words helped me feel I was not alone, I still was stalled by how my adoptive mother would react. This one felt like a double whammy. She could see my decision to search as betrayal. I am also very cognizant I've shared some less-than-perfect depictions of my childhood and how she comes across in those stories. Portraying her as a monster is not my intention. She is not one, but the words I've used in some cases may offer different imagery.

We had our share of difficulties and did not always agree. Despite the chaos, and the critical approach she sometimes employed, I love her very much. I am incredibly grateful she wanted me and chose me.

I recognize she did not have the easiest of lives, yet she always did her best to prioritize her children. She worked a full-time job and was the sole caretaker for me and my sister until I was almost nine. She always made sure we had proper childcare and mostly had us stay with family members or close neighbors while she worked. Up until her death at eighty-one years old, she remained totally self-sufficient and a survivor throughout her life.

When she married John, she still worked full time and took care of the house and us. John helped, too, but he worked nights, so things like dinner and homework were her responsibility at the end of an already long day.

My clashes with my mom were a result of her survivalist tendencies and pattern of codependency. She had to fight for her own life in so many ways; therefore, she was very defensive at times. Her protective walls were quite thick, and when she felt hurt or not seen, she lashed out. What is interesting is I learned and repeated these patterns in my own life. She softened over the years, but I still saw her revert when she felt threatened in some way.

My mom had polio as a little girl, so things were difficult for her from the very start. She had heart disease from a young age as well and survived a few major heart surgeries. Her hardened tendencies are understandable, but when I was a young girl, her curt and direct nature pushing me to be strong left me with some scars.

Reading the stories about the adoptees in Pam's book made me realize we all have our own struggles. While I have emotional scars and have experienced some trauma in my life, things still turned out well for me.

I have arrived at a place in my life where I acknowledge I am the only one responsible for my actions and reactions. I made a conscious choice to keep the information about searching for and finding my biological family to myself until I was ready to share. I was once again reminded of my mother's decision to wait. I now understood her need to hold off until the "right time."

I wanted to be more settled with the events that had been transpiring. I also wanted to tell her in person. She was living in Florida, so that needed to be planned.

At first, I questioned if I was holding back to make her comfortable. I was not. By waiting, I gave myself the time I needed to process all I had learned and experienced. My intention was to be fully present with her and be able to take care of whatever her reaction was. That's why I needed the time to make it right with myself.

Overall, in my life I desire to be authentic and speak my truth. I am not always successful because I also want to please others so they will love and accept me. This contradiction can create some messy interactions.

I chose a different way this time. I embraced this story and my version of this truth. At times, I might have a distorted recollection of what really happened. However, if that is how I remember it, then it stays with me as a memory that occurred as I described it.

By openly sharing these situations and how they impacted my life, I reclaimed a sense of power and freedom. I own my participation in the negative aspects of my life, but I can no longer allow myself to take responsibility for the behavior and reactions of others. Hopefully by witnessing my path, others can also see a new way to handle and clear old patterns.

I did finally have that conversation with my adoptive mom, and she was supportive and protective in the best way possible.

I went to visit her in December 2022, and I stayed the night at her place. I started the conversation like the ripping of a Band-Aid, quite similar to the conversation she and I had in January 1992 in her kitchen.

I blurted out, "Mom, I found my biological family this summer, and I want to share what happened."

It took her a minute to digest what I had just dumped on her, but she bounced back quickly and displayed genuine interest.

I quickly told her about the interaction with my biological sister, "Don't worry, Mom, my biological mother and her family want nothing to do with me."

Her mama bear instincts kicked in, "What do you mean? How could they not want anything to do with you? That's ridiculous."

I read her anger toward my biological mother as protection and felt her body relax as she took in this piece of critical information. She wanted me to have everything and carried the fear of losing me, even now. She asked lots of questions.

It was honestly one of my most beautiful experiences with her yet. We processed together, and she shared some details with me we had not previously discussed, for whatever reason.

She reflected, "I remembered something about your father when your biological mother was asked about his whereabouts. She indicated he was too young and would not be involved."

My mother sat in silence for a few moments as if she was transported back to 1967 reliving that time but through the lens of our current relationship.

Since then, we've gone back and rewritten some of our stories together. Recently I called and read some of the sentiments about her I shared in this book, and she was genuinely touched.

She shared, "When you tell me these things, I heal too."

Hearing her use those words was unbelievable. This has certainly softened the blow of my biological family's continued denial of my existence.

I still toggle back and forth between the guilt of my search and what I've shared, especially about my childhood. However, if I redact these relevant pieces of information, I am participating in the layered complexity of shame and secrets that fuel my story. Moving forward would be almost impossible if I held on to the baggage of my past.

Through the book *Reunited*, I am reminded I am not alone in this situation. Reading the stories of others and hearing Pam's insights reassure me we are all on our own journey, and mine is no worse or better than anyone else's. I physically felt pain and sadness while reading about others' reunions. Not comparing my outcome to theirs is hard. Pam has led her clients to many happy outcomes, even the ones that didn't look promising in the beginning.

I have a loving story with my biological father's side, but the grave disappointment of the repeated rejection from my biological mother's family continued to suffocate me. We live so close to each other, yet she has not made any attempt to meet me. I hoped after they had time to think about it, they would reach out, but as of this writing, it had been nine months with no response.

LET IT BE
One of the stories Pam shares is about a biological father who looked for his daughter her whole life. He was not given any input on the decision by the mother when she went away and gave their baby up for adoption (Slaton 2012, 122–143).

That story made me think about my biological dad. *What would he have done if he had known about me? Would my grandmother have ended up raising me?* When I spoke with my aunt recently, we briefly touched on this subject.

I jokingly said to her, "Maybe you would have ended up raising me."

She chuckled in response. We don't think my biological mom ever gave my biological father the opportunity to have any input on the decision.

When the father in Pam's story found his daughter, he overwhelmed her. She was reluctant since she had not been the one searching. That was a big reminder for me. Everyone deserves the space and time to process what this means to them. I am living this, working through all the pieces, and I am sensitive to how this shows up for others who are impacted by or involved in my story.

However, I am human and can't hide because they want to pretend I am not real. I have given thought to reaching out again to my biological mother's family. At the time of this writing, I have not yet made any further moves to do so.

Each situation is unique and has layers. For a long time, I thought no one understood how I felt. Now I see that is not true.

Pam speaks of this very obstacle I struggle with:

The other obstacle people face in their search is the loyalty issue. So many adoptees are afraid of hurting their adoptive parents. They live in fear that if they choose to meet their birth family, they will make the ones they love most—the people who raised them—feel inadequate or threatened (Slaton 2012, Introduction).

It is like she is in my head, reading my innermost thoughts.

She reacts to her own comment with, "If a parent can love more than one child, why can't a child love more than one parent?" (Slaton 2012, Introduction).

The undercurrent for adoptees to want to know our roots and understand our DNA is strong. How can we ground in our own lives without fully understanding the roots of our own origin?

While this seems like a fair and rational case, I had a lot of uncertainty and a level of fear about how it would be received by my adoptive mom.

Pam says, "The need to connect is especially intense when it comes to our birth mothers. It's an organic bond that's always there. You were in this person's womb. No matter what happens, you are her flesh and blood, and it will always feel like a piece of you is missing without her acknowledgment. That feeling stays close to the surface your whole life" (Slaton 2012, 5).

In Chapter 2 of Pam's book, she shares one of her most difficult cases. A successful Texan businessman who had the means and the desire but kept hitting roadblocks every way he turned. He was trying to find his biological mother. When they finally found her, she declined meeting him. She had never told her family, and she had concern about a secret of this nature being unearthed so many years later. At least she had the decency to share why she didn't feel she could meet him. I read this story a few times, and each time I found myself sobbing. She eventually agreed to meet him once, and during that meeting shared his biological father's information. He sought out his father, and ironically his father was thrilled to learn about him and meet him. He ended up fostering a strong relationship with his biological dad and brothers (Slaton 2012, 18–35).

I share this anecdote because ultimately we have zero insight about how any of the players in our stories will react. This one client of hers had deep tenacity and would not take no for an answer. I got one Facebook message from my biological sister, and I shut it down on my end. I could have reached out to my other siblings, but I didn't. I am not completely sure why I stopped there. I've thought often about writing a letter to my biological mother and have toyed with the idea of sending her this book when it's published. In this moment, I've chosen to pause. It will be determined later if I reach out again.

When I read or hear other stories about reunions, especially biological siblings, my throat closes, and my heart feels constricted. While I didn't expect they would roll out the red carpet, I thought maybe curiosity would take over and they would at least meet me for coffee or have a phone call. I assume my approach hampered the possibility of a warm welcome, but I also am not sure how I contacted them mattered.

I have thought, "I am not going to chase them." *Is that my ego protecting me or my higher self preserving me? Or both?*

After reading about others, I am reminded sometimes you need to be more persistent or tenacious. I may be taking this stance of not chasing to protect my heart.

For now, I revel in the progress I've made and what I've learned in less than one year, and I continue to take care of myself. Self-care remains a key aspect to my growth and forward movement.

CHAPTER 11

AWARENESS AND INTENTION CREATE SELF-CONNECTION

My life has evolved from being reactive and crisis driven to being intentional and values driven. I realized I had cloaked myself in avoidance, through busyness, overscheduling, and numbing tendencies of overindulgent behavior. I used to brag that I worked hard and played hard. On the outside it appeared I had everything I wished for, but on the inside, I felt unworthy and never enough, consistently chasing something.

Awareness was a gift that arose through healing work. Many small changes resulted in big shifts for me. By connecting inward and listening to my heart, I was able to level up my thinking and, ultimately, my life.

Once I realized energy work, coaching, and overall spiritual heath were not a once-a-week practice, transformation occurred. My first coach in 2013, before Lara, initiated our work together by telling me I needed to meditate and have a morning practice. I scoffed at that, literally. It didn't feel likely for me, nor could I relate.

Currently, I still don't have a routine that involves a set morning practice, but I have tools, modalities, and a knowledge base I actively access to help me cope with upsets when they arise. I have a mindset focused on growth and self-care. Some days I start with meditation or affirmations, indicating a more regular practice is on the precipice of emerging. The lessons don't subside; our ability to address them is what elevates. I've accepted one size does not fit all. This type of work is personal, and certain things will resonate more with some than others. An open-minded approach will allow you to find what's best for you.

In this Chapter I introduce a few of the many tools that have become meaningful for me. Many of the concepts I have been exposed to and adopted have been around for thousands of years. Nothing I present here is new, nor of my own creation.

How I integrated these into my life makes them unique for me.

INTENTIONS
At the beginning of 2020 I declared it my "Year of Intention." Each month I set a different intention and aimed to build a practice around it.

Below is an outline of that endeavor:

- January: Be present. Practice mindfulness: Recognize that time is a gift.
- February: Commit to consistency.
- March: Celebrate the wins: big and small.
- April: Self: Awareness, acceptance, compassion; Take notice of self-talk.
- May: Movement, physical and in life. (Transitions can be hard; movement can be scary.)
- June: Be curious and open to new possibilities.
- July: Freedom to choose; Take note of what and who influences me.
- August: Feel what needs to heal.
- September: Focus. What you give energy to inevitably grows. Elevate your self-care game.
- October: Create your future.
- November: Practice gratitude. Expect little. Give much.
- December: Every end is a new beginning. Let go. Surrender.

Obviously when the year started, I had no idea we would find ourselves in a pandemic and on lockdown for a significant amount of time. The importance of this practice was heightened and gave me strength during times of deep isolation and lack of human interaction. I stayed the course with the Year of Intention, and it enabled me to make significant strides in my self-care and healing goals.

A few examples of how I applied these intentions within my life were:

January's intention was to be present. I used to pride myself on being a multitasker. I came to realize I never truly engaged in one thing, because I was splitting my energy across many things at once and always felt frazzled, overwhelmed, and often disappointed.

When I started to work on being present, I experienced how powerful mindfulness is.

Whenever someone recommended meditation, I rolled my eyes and commented, "That's not for me; I am not a meditator."

What does that even mean? My instinct was to resist. It felt uncomfortable. Meditation was for the yoga studio, and I was not a yogi.

I was wrong.

Meditation is an incredible gift and tool. It calms the mind and body, enhances focus, and reduces stress. I mainly practice through guided meditations, with someone talking you through the exercise either live or recorded. In the beginning, I fell asleep every single time. My self-talk said I was meditating wrong, which is not possible, by the way. I felt different afterward, even if I was asleep for most of the exercise. I was calmer, focused, and open to ideas and creativity. My subconscious did not need to be awake to receive the benefits.

If I was trying to solve a problem and took a break to meditate, I came back with a broader lens of what was possible. If I was upset about something and couldn't let go of it, a greater propensity for forgiveness or letting go typically blossomed. I love meditation now, and while it is still not a daily practice, I will stop to meditate when I need to calm my nervous system or shift something I can't seem to shake.

The second part of this intention was to practice mindfulness, the act of being specifically present. This can be applied in every aspect of your life. Mindful eating is often referenced and reminds us to be engaged during a meal instead of sitting in front of the television or computer while wolfing down a sandwich at lunch. It encourages us to get up and walk away to revitalize ourselves and our energy.

When preparing a meal, you can strive to notice the colors, the texture, and the smell. Mindfulness invites you to fully engage in the sensory aspects of what you are doing. By being mindful, you can feel less scattered and more directed.

The last part is about embracing the value of time. By recognizing time is a gift, we start to protect it with more intention. This was meaningful for me. I had always been running or jumping from one thing to another on my never-ending to-do list. I set myself up for failure most days, trying to get through all the things that needed to get done and ultimately felt deflated or disappointed with my lack of results.

By living with intention, I proactively think about how I want to feel throughout my days. Who do I want to surround myself with? I consider what and who invites or represents joy. I work to make sure I am doing what helps me achieve these standards. I protect my energy and invoke boundaries when necessary.

I did not do any of these things before. As I began to create a new way of life, changes gradually occurred.

In February my intention was to commit to consistency. I still have not mastered this one. I've always resisted structure and told myself it was too stifling. I have the same negative association with the word "discipline." Both words make me feel limited and confined. However, structure and discipline are necessary elements of any practice, whether it's exercise, meditation, sleep, nutrition, or any aspect of self-care. By committing to consistency, I recognized I needed the structure, and I changed both my mindset and actions. I achieved considerable growth by this mindset shift.

To commit to consistency, I had to prioritize myself, which was scary. Old stories about being selfish blared loudly in my head. *How could I make time for myself when so much else needed to get done?* My default setting always prioritized work. My to-do list was forever interminable, yet I strived daily to finish it. The cycle perpetuated: cross two things off and add three more. I never had enough time.

I made a small tweak to my approach and scheduled workouts, walks, meditations, or whatever else I decided was important enough to preserve the time to ensure it happened. A big mindset shift occurred. I was important enough! What I wanted to do mattered, and when I put it in the calendar, it happened. No one got upset. It wasn't the end of the world if everything on the to-do list didn't get done. Oh, and if someone did get upset, that was their issue, not mine. I don't mean that in a confrontational, entitled way. I finally recognized making space for the things that helped me had long-lasting effects for everyone involved.

Each of these intentions provided me with the ability to focus on a specific aspect of self-care, growth, and healing. By agreeing to live intentionally and in alignment through these monthly dedications, my lack-based consciousness changed. I was not as worried about the other shoe falling. When something did happen, I was equipped to handle it and had the confidence to address it.

I was safe and connected to myself.

CHAKRAS
In my work with Lara, she often talked about chakras. Through her I developed a basic knowledge of chakras, but I was fascinated and wanted to learn more. If you've done yoga, practiced meditation, or participated in any Reiki or energy healing, you have likely heard of chakras.

Chakras are energy centers that run through your body. I love them because I can relate to the basic principles, and they make it easy for me to create my own road map of self-care and further understand the energy in my body. I have grown to be able to pinpoint when energy is blocked in a certain area and know how to address it. This is the work Lara had done for me. I still work with her, but I have developed the capability of reading myself, and that is powerful.

Much information on this very ancient concept exists, but for our purpose I've provided a rudimentary outline of each one based on my own interpretation and the usefulness of chakras in my life.

As I mentioned, when I worked with Lara we often focused on a spot where my energy was stuck, and she was able to determine whether it was a chakra or something else.

Lara would say, "Your solar plexus is blown." Or, "That blew your throat chakra."

Both of those examples indicate my body was out of alignment with a thought, feeling, or meaning I've given to something.

The seven energy centers are:

- Root Chakra—"Instinctual Need for Survival": being grounded and feeling safe.
- Sacral Chakra—"Pleasure Seeker": seeking playfulness, creativity, owning your sexuality, and pleasure center.
- Solar Plexus Chakra—"Power Driver": understanding your personal power and identity.
- Heart Chakra—"Searching for Love": love for yourself, others, and setting loving boundaries. Also connects the upper three and lower three chakras.
- Throat Chakra—"Expressing Your Truth": finding your voice and speaking your truth.
- Third Eye Chakra—"Transcending Beyond Ego": being open to new experiences and your future and connecting to your higher self and future self.

- Crown Chakra—"Spiritual Awakening": connecting to source, accessing your intuition, and divine guidance.

The more I learned and applied to my own life and healing, the more I wanted to know. The more I knew, the more I grew. People commented on changes they witnessed in me. My anger was no longer in charge. I had the gift of knowledge and awareness. I had tools to help me manage when upsets occurred because they certainly did and still do.

AFFIRMATIONS

The chakras provided a beautiful foundation. I started out by making intentional choices about my life and how I chose to spend my days. Then I paid attention to my energy and how each of the possibilities in my daily life made me feel. Recognizing the elements of chakras and being able to adjust my reactions to certain circumstances and conditions disrupted things in a very positive way. Next, I learned how to reinforce and claim positivity.

Cue the next step as I developed my practice.

Affirmations are positive statements that remind us we are okay when we are feeling anxious, overwhelmed, unsure, scared, or any other negative emotion. Affirmations reinforce a positive belief or feeling when we need it most.

They do not have to be tied to chakras, but for this exercise the following affirmations do.

I AM SAFE AND SECURE: ROOT CHAKRA

Getting clear on what being safe meant removed another huge boulder blocking me from progression. When I anticipate a fight-or-flight situation, I ground myself. To be grounded means you can feel yourself on stable footing. You can literally take off your shoes and feel the earth beneath your feet if you choose. Other ways I ground myself: Breathe in essential oils, tap certain points to calm my nervous system, get still (meditation), and breathe.

While performing one of the above, I tell myself I am safe, and I am secure. My body calms, and I am reassured I am not in danger.

While writing this book, it went through heavy edits, and I often found myself deeply immersed in the emotion of the content. Old wounds were resurrected. I was feeling raw and exposed. I have a five-minute meditation I really enjoy and listen to often. When I felt the work getting too intense, I paused, played that meditation (sometimes twice), and then breathed in some lemon oil. The whole sequence took about twelve minutes, and I felt ready for the rest of the day. By taking time for that practice, I totally shifted my energy.

I EMBRACE MY CREATIVITY AND PLAYFUL SIDE: SACRAL CHAKRA

Play is something I had abandoned for many years. I buried my creativity and playfulness with responsibility and obligations to my business, family, friends, and pretty much anything except myself. I believed if I took my eye off the ball, something would undoubtedly fall apart. It became so apparent to me I had deserted my goofy and playful side.

Returning to this lighter side didn't mean I was irresponsible; it simply meant I allowed time to reconnect to fun. These days you might find me telling jokes in a meeting. Or I may blast my inspirational songs for a break between meetings and dance it out.

Adventure is part of play and curiosity. Travel fuels that aspect, and I take the opportunity to change up my scenery as often as possible. People react to my travel, and I've learned that is a mirror for themselves. I don't have to apologize for my lifestyle nor my love of travel and connection.

**I STAND IN MY POWER. I ACCEPT MYSELF:
SOLAR PLEXUS CHAKRA**

I stopped blaming others for things that are happening or not in my life. I allowed my true self to emerge, despite how others react to that identity. The solar plexus is your power center and is physically located in your gut area. This chakra typically governs your instincts and intuition. The more I connected to my own identity and power center, the more confident and directed I became. Living intentionally is easier when my solar plexus is in alignment.

**MY HEART KNOWS WHAT I WANT AND NEED,
AND I LISTEN: HEART CHAKRA**

I am listening to my heart. When it tells me I need something, I listen with intention, understanding my heart's needs, how to prioritize them, and how to take care of myself and not rely so much on others for love and acceptance. I accept myself.

I SPEAK MY TRUTH: THROAT CHAKRA

I do my best to speak with love and compassion, even in difficult conversations. If I am not being treated fairly, I address the situation. I tell people how they make me feel, both good and bad. If something is worth fighting for, I speak up, and I ask for what I need.

I AM OPEN TO DIVINE GUIDANCE AND LIFE'S ENDLESS POSSIBILITIES: THIRD EYE CHAKRA

I am open to the possibilities the future holds, knowing I can trust myself. I embrace my higher and future self. I trust the universe and divine guidance. I know I am protected and guided. The universe has amazing things in store for me, and I don't have to work so hard to control the outcome.

I know who I am, I know what I am, and I know how I serve.

I embrace the possibilities of all that is ahead of me, and I know my value. I am enough. I have enough. I am safe. I am experienced. Of all the lessons, at the core, my ability to feel and know I am safe is the most prominent. Knowing I am secure gives me the strength I need to keep moving forward. I am ready, and I can trust myself to make the best decisions for me, despite how others may react.

I AM ONE WITH ALL THAT IS: CROWN CHAKRA

I am not alone. This was a huge breakthrough for me, considering abandonment was at the core of almost every story I had attached to my life. I trust I am guided and protected.

I move from a place of inspired action. This shift feels magical, and my future is full of promise.

These guiding principles have provided me with a solid foundation. I shifted from a survival-based mentality, operating from a place of scarcity, to a safety-based approach, where I work from abundance and love. I have a purpose and I am beyond grateful for that special gift.

HOW YOU CAN BENEFIT FROM THESE TOOLS
I hope something here resonated enough for you to consider further exploration. Allow yourself to connect inward and leave space to be curious, open, and trust your instincts. Magic will follow!

Try the meditation, affirmations, and chakra-related tools mentioned here. If none of these call out to you, don't fret. In the world of healing, self-connection, and living intentionally, you can find something that will be relatable to you.

I invite you to give yourself room to play and discover different types of healing, self-care, and personal development. The journey of exploration is an incredibly powerful gift. You deserve to try it out. I feel very confident you will find something that fits your lifestyle, mindset, and learning style. Remember, this is an ongoing practice, so be patient with yourself.

Little by little, we can make incredible changes in our lives.

> Be present. Be mindful. Be cognizant of the
> gift of time. Be consistent. Be intentional.

CHAPTER 12

LET GO OF SHAME, KNOW WHEN TO SURRENDER

Now that you are listening with mastery, are you shocked and appalled to hear how you speak to yourself? Would you speak to your friend or loved one that way? How can you operate from a place of higher self more consistently? Can you even connect to the concept of higher self, or is your ego still in charge?

Let's assume you have stepped forward as your true self and are speaking your heart's desires. Does that feel authentic or are you anxious? Where are you feeling stuck? Are you able to stay in your power and clearly ask for what you want? If you are, do you end up retreating in shame or guilt? Are you second-guessing yourself after the fact?

You've made strides to be more intentional. Self-care is more prominent in your daily routine, and you are making time to try new things, possibly even the ones offered in the prior chapter.

You are moving along and feel like you've got a handle on this stuff, then *bam,* something knocks you off course. You revert to that nasty self-talk. *You aren't good enough. You never stick with anything. Why did you think this was for you? You are not one of those touchy-feely people! When will you ever learn?*

Throughout this book I've introduced some terms and concepts that have been life altering for me. I tend to obsess over definitions because I need to ensure all parties are speaking the same language when engaging in conversation or collaboration.

Words are powerful, and they stick with us. They are more than just letters on a piece of paper, or components of a sentence. Words create stories, which instill beliefs, resulting in behaviors that ultimately foster outcomes.

The words, phrases, and concepts that come next, along with the ones we've already touched on, have been pivotal to the shift that transpired for me. I am fraught over how best to describe these terms so they would be meaningful and universally embraced. Left to interpretation, words like shame, guilt, surrender, or self-care are open to multiple definitions. This affects our ability to have a unified conversation and maintain a mutual understanding of our experiences.

SHAME AND GUILT

Brené Brown is an expert on shame and has been studying it for decades. She speaks often on this topic. Until hearing her, I didn't use the word "shame" a lot. However, I experienced it all the time. I now realize shame had me emotionally persecuted for many crimes I didn't commit.

In her TED talk on shame and guilt, she says, "Shame drives two big tapes— 'never good enough,' and, if you can talk it out of that one, 'who do you think you are?' The thing to understand about shame is, it's not guilt. Shame is a focus on self; guilt is a focus on behavior. Shame is 'I am bad.' Guilt is 'I did something bad'" (Brown 2012).

The online introduction for that TED talk reads, "Shame is an unspoken epidemic, the secret behind many forms of broken behavior. Brené Brown, whose earlier talk on vulnerability became a viral hit, explores what can happen when people confront their shame head-on" (Brown 2012).

The thought of shame being an epidemic really struck me, especially the perspective of the secrets driving the broken behavior. This was absolutely the case for me. Realizing I could let go of shame was freeing, even if others were clenching to it with tight fists and committed to wallowing in it.

Part of my own healing journey has included various aspects of spiritual exploration. One of my best friends is a Reiki master, and I've done many sessions with her. Once we complete the work, she provides feedback on what came up.

This one time she shared, "I saw your biological mother, and she was pregnant with you. Everyone around her was telling her why she couldn't keep this child. She was so defeated. She didn't have any support."

If your belief system supports the notion that we hear what's happening while we are in our mother's womb, then one of the first things I heard was I was a burden to my mother. Coupled with the present-day denial by her again, I am encapsulated by shame, and it started even before I was born. I believe the shame my mother carried was energetically passed to me.

That shame spiral continued throughout my birth, childhood, teenage, and adult life. With awareness, I feel awakened about how shame attaches to us and affects us subconsciously, dominating our thoughts and contributing to our feelings of unworthiness.

SURRENDER
Conversely, let's talk about surrender, a word that has become a beacon of guidance as my spiritual journey unfolded. Only in the past year have I been able to embrace the act of surrender. As I thought about what surrender means and how best to impart a unified definition to my readers, I got stuck in a bit of a perfectionist loop. I went through this entire iteration of googling "surrender" and trying to find the perfect definition.

Each definition or search result left me disappointed and dismayed. I kept trying.

What does it mean when you surrender spiritually? What does it mean to surrender in a relationship? What's the difference between surrendering and quitting?

My brain interjected, *Of course you can't find the perfect definition. Why do you keep trying to write the perfect book?*

Great, now, that you-are-not-good-enough tape was playing on repeat. Followed by, "What makes you an expert on surrender?"

Well, here's the thing. I am not an expert, nor do I have to be. My expertise is in my own experience and what learning to surrender has allowed me to do. Surrender is recognizing when a situation or an outcome is completely out of your control. You are clear on what you want, but you have no idea how it may come to fruition. At that point you hand it over to a higher power. One of my coaches refers to this as Gus—God, Universe, Source. However you approach this, remembering you can let go of the need to control the outcome is important.

Surrender is not giving up or quitting. It is relinquishing the control, worry, doubt, fear, anxiety, and whatever other tapes your brain attaches to these "looped" situations.

If something is meant for you, it will find its way. Consider a job or a project you really want. If you've done all the work, interviewed at your best, sent in impeccable references, and demonstrated your capabilities, at that point you surrender. As we talked about in an earlier chapter, "Rejection is protection." If for some reason the job does not come to you, likely a better opportunity awaits.

I have heard the word surrender used when referring to a mother deciding to put their child up for adoption. The phrases I've been using throughout this book have been "given up" or "gave away." To think "she surrendered me to a possible better life" feels more comforting.

In that version of the story, I focus on the grace of her surrender and release myself of all the stories that make me not good enough or not worthy of her love. I surrender my need for her and my biological siblings to accept me, invite me, or welcome me into their family.

I could not control how my mother handled her pregnancy with me before I was born, and I could not control how they reacted to my attempt to connect with them. I hold compassion for my biological mother and accept she didn't quit on me. She made sure I went to a good family and did what she believed to be best for me, given her circumstances.

When the circumstances are beyond our control, we can choose to release the shame and blame. We let go and surrender.

CHAPTER 13

NEW DATA. NEW STORY.

All the data supporting my old story—"people leave after they get to know me"—has been rendered irrelevant. I am no longer attached to that story and have new evidence demonstrating how loved and supported I am. Does that mean I never experience feelings of abandonment, letdown, or disappointment? Of course not!

In late 2022, a situation at work arose that catapulted me back into that abandonment story, and it was as if I had forgotten all the growth I had experienced. Thankfully it didn't last for long, but nonetheless it happened.

When I sold my company, I stayed on with the acquiring firm as a full-time employee for almost three years. I was actively considering my next chapter, but I was not fully ready to leave. They generously allowed me to transition to a consulting role. A little over a year later, that contract was renegotiated, and the updated proposed contract reduced both my responsibilities and compensation significantly. This was not what I was expecting, and I flashed back to the old story of not being enough. I thought now they knew the real me, they wanted me out.

How could I no longer be needed?

This felt ironic because I had brought in a roster of clients that we successfully retained. I had been transitioning those clients to other team members internally over the past two years, work done in preparation to allow me to build other aspects of the business.

My intention was not to make myself obsolete. Now I felt displaced and went into panic mode. *Why did I let them take the clients? Why did I give up my control? Why did I sell my business?*

What was confusing for me, and likely others, was I had consistently expressed the desire to pursue other interests outside of the IT space. I talked about coaching, writing a book, and offering retreats. From that viewpoint, this reduction was a blessing. It gave me more time to focus on the things I wanted to build, explore areas I had not had time to discover, follow my dream to be an author, and serve a community through coaching. It allowed me to maintain my passion for travel and connection, which I had started to cultivate over the past year.

However, since this change did not happen how I perceived it needed to for me to feel safe and supported, I recoiled and reverted to my old behaviors. I canceled workouts an hour before I was supposed to meet with my trainer, time that was sacred to me and I had prioritized. I boomeranged back to old patterns and thought sequences. I was hiding and scared. My financial safety net had been removed, right when I was at the midway point of my tightrope walk.

It was my intention to move on to other things. Then I realized I was still trying to prove myself. I was still seeking validation. The fact I had successfully started, grown, and sold a company and retained most of the customers throughout the transition didn't quiet the critical voices in my head. I was in survival mode.

And then I remembered, I didn't need anyone to reassure me I was capable. I am capable. I am qualified. With that reminder, I flipped the script. Instead of: "I am not enough, I am not valued," or, "No one cares about my needs," I embraced the pause. I'd been given a gift of time. I was grateful for all they had done for me and for the space I'd been given during this time of transition.

I created other projects and possibilities without feeling guilty that I wasn't prioritizing this client and their needs. My sense of urgency shifted. My purpose moved to the top of the list. I left no room for avoidance and procrastination. That incessant need to fill my calendar with busyness and seeking approval from others dissipated.

I was free and ready for the next adventure.

REWRITING MY STORY SPARKED NEW BEGINNINGS
Over the course of my twenty-year IT business, many of my clients became friends. After four years of not being the

owner, I still have incredible relationships and connections with several of them. They got to know me and didn't leave. That certainly felt like new data.

Throughout the pages of this book, I've narrated stories that spoke specifically to either adoption stories or folks that have shown up to support me in times of need. I wish I could write about every single person who has influenced me and made a difference in my life. I have been so blessed with many great friends, influencers, mentors, and supporters.

As I thought about this concept of new data to support a new story, I considered friendships that had traversed several decades and withstood challenging circumstances.

When my family left New York in 1986, I was a freshman at Baruch College. I met someone who went on to play a very significant role in my life and is still one of my best friends today. She had an established group, consisting of her childhood bestie, who grew up across the street from her, and two close friends she met in high school. Being a fifth wheel among four women who knew each other so well felt like a terrible idea to me, based on my prior experiences, but I liked her. They accepted me and made me feel like I belonged from the onset.

My friendship with these four incredible women has spanned almost four decades, surviving my move to Florida, marriages, divorces, kids, loss of parents, and so many life-affecting moments. I know their parents, spouses, in-laws, siblings, nieces, nephews, and other relatives. I have known all their kids since birth and have celebrated many milestones with all of them.

I am fortunate to say there are several stories like this one. Each one presents evidence that people stick around. That does not mean there are not conflicts to resolve or times when struggles exist. Life and relationships can be messy.

At this point in my life, I value the depth and the history of all my friends. I truly appreciate those who stuck by me, even when the way I acted did not necessarily deem me worthy of their friendship. Alcohol plagued much of those rough times. I would get drunk and be difficult, confrontational, and downright mean.

One friend I am still very close with would candidly call me out on my behavior, and I didn't always like it, but I loved her and still do. When she gave me feedback, I listened. Through those not-so-easy conversations I learned how others saw me, and at that time, it was not in a good way. I worked to figure out what made me that way and sought to improve. For those friends to still be so close in my life and to have them witness and experience my growth is a gift. I am so grateful they have all been such an integral part of my journey and story.

FEAR: FALSE EVIDENCE APPEARING REAL
Have you ever seen this acronym for FEAR: False Evidence Appearing Real?

Remember the monsters in your closet or under your bed when you were growing up? Those were fears we fabricated in the form of monsters hiding or lurking, out of plain sight. We could not see them, but they took up space in our minds and made us feel unsafe. I have had multiple versions of monsters in my closet or under my bed for most of my life, with varying degrees of fear attached to them.

I had a complicated relationship with fear, and it interrupted certain aspects of my life. After 9/11 I had not flown solo. I love to travel and try to do it often. Prior to 9/11 I had traveled via airplane plenty of times to destinations both near and far. After experiencing the trauma of that day, I no longer felt safe flying alone for fear I would have a panic attack, or the plane would be hijacked. I was on the ground in NYC that day, but my business partner was on a plane, and I was scheduled to fly that afternoon. Our office was very close to the World Trade Center, and my experience left me with unresolved trauma for almost two decades.

Whenever I had to go anywhere, for business or leisure, I set it up so I traveled with someone. It was incredibly limiting, but it was the only way I could fly. I am especially grateful to my colleague Jess, who did a lot of extra traveling to accommodate me and my limitations during that time.

In 2018, I had a very special reunion planned with college friends, a group of women I met in St. Augustine at Flagler College in 1992. Some of us had not seen each other in twenty-five years, so this was a big deal. For this trip to Key West, I did not have anyone I could fly with. The girls were coming from Long Beach, California, and Atlanta, and two were already in Florida. If I wanted to be at this reunion, I had to fly by myself.

I faced my fear. I found no direct flights to Key West, so I flew through Atlanta and met my friend who lives there so we could travel to Key West together. I had not seen her since 1996. All I had to do was get from LaGuardia Airport in New York City to Atlanta. I worked with Lara on clearing my fears around this. My understanding of how critical the need to feel safe deepened. This was another breakthrough moment for me.

We worked on False Evidence Appearing Real. The fact terrorists had hijacked four planes on 9/11 and crashed all of them was real, but I could not control what would happen when I was on this flight.

This was reminiscent of fourteen-year-old me dreaming of crashing into the Atlantic Ocean while flying from New York to Arizona. My fear was irrational, but it was enough to cause me to create situations where I felt protected or at least not alone. Being on an airplane with no one to look out for me and being abandoned in an emergency with no one to save me was probably my deepest fear at that time.

I had not slept much the night before, a habit I still have today. If I have an early morning flight, I typically stay up the night before to deal with my anxiety about traveling by myself. I left in the morning for the airport, and my heart was racing from the moment I ordered the Uber. Oddly, I don't remember the specifics of the flight from NYC. I flew Delta Air Lines and bought a first-class ticket. I felt I needed to be closer to the flight attendants should something go wrong. But I don't remember any details of the actual flight, just that I was incredibly anxious to arrive in Atlanta.

When I finally got to the gate for our flight to Key West, I saw my friend, and we instantly were in that comfortable flow of friendship I so fondly remember from our college days. She is the core of our group in many ways. We all look up to her, and she has a way of making us all feel seen, heard, and acknowledged. Often, she is our bartender and our driver, but for me, she makes me feel safe and grounds me. I think she grounds all of us.

For the next forty-eight hours, we were back in a place where we had so many happy memories. The reunion was amazing, and I am glad I didn't let my fear of flying alone stop me from being there that weekend. I knew when we met in 1992, this was a special group of women. The gift of finding each other and reigniting that light of friendship over twenty-five years later is one thing I don't take for granted.

Seeing it through the lens of False Evidence Appearing Real, I established a new relationship with fear.

NEW EVIDENCE WHICH WAS REAL
These stories and the ones I have not shared demonstrate my fears of abandonment and being left out, which were my own monsters in my closet and under my bed. I am not a perfect friend or person, but I have so much evidence that says I am a friend worth sticking around for.

If you know me personally, please understand you are a part of my journey, and my story, even if I did not specifically mention you. I value every person who influenced me along the way. If we've lost touch, that does not mean what we shared does not still mean something to me. I have learned and grown from every person I have had in my life. I am better for knowing you and having had you as a part of my story.

I would like to leave each one of you, whether you know me or not, with this thought: *What or who are the monsters under your bed or in your closet? What is False Evidence Appearing Real keeping you from doing?*

I encourage you to look for new data in your life that tells a different story than an old one you might still be holding on to. Where are the friendships in your life that have weathered the storms? What are the things you've accomplished that you've allowed to be overshadowed by stories that no longer serve you?

CHAPTER 14

SAFE AT LAST

All I ever wanted was to feel safe. That is what most of us want.

To ensure that my assumption was correct, I asked others what being safe meant to them.

Maria shared, "Feeling safe for me looks like enough money in the bank, a safe place to live, low crime, and feeling loved and appreciated by my nearest and dearest."

Eden said, "Feeling safe means trusting those I love, money in the bank, and a journey with my loved one next to me."

Gina responded, "Feeling safe to me means being vulnerable and comfortable to be my true self."

Tawnya elaborated, "Safe is a feeling for me. I feel comforted, held, and relaxed. No constriction. I can show up completely as myself with no judgment."

First of all, I love that these dear friends felt safe enough to share their responses when I asked for their input. I agree with all and continue to dig deeper to clearly define my own meaning of safety.

Safety is a feeling for me too. It is about being centered and grounded. Safety is a recognition that everything is going to be okay, even in times of upset or turmoil. One time I was driving to Vermont, and I ended up on this mountain trail. The ground was covered in snow and ice, and I lost signal. It was almost dark, and I mindfully focused on staying calm and trusting I would find my way back. If I let my anxiety take the wheel, I could have furthered the possible danger. By staying centered and grounded, I was able to find a safe place to turn around and return down the mountain before dark. That was a noticeable moment of understanding how important feeling safe is to me.

I took a course to gain a deeper understanding of the chakras. I was incredibly drawn to the root chakra. The root chakra is our foundation and is all about feeling safe and secure. It develops during our first seven years of life and deals with survival and security. It's represented by the color red, and when out of balance, we might feel insecure, unsafe, on shaky ground, and even disconnected from reality.

The first seven years of my life had a major impact on my own sense of security and safety. My mother did try to keep me safe, but we had a lot of unsettled moments during those formative years. This concept of feeling grounded was introduced to me in 2014 when I started energy work. In 2020 it was reinforced deeply and provided the foundation I needed to move forward to find my biological family and level up my growth.

Knowing I am on solid ground is a barometer to how I measure how safe I feel in a situation. Recognizing when I need to ground and how to do so have become incredibly powerful tools for me. Thinking about being safe, I went back to the acronym of FEAR, and how seeing it broken down that way encouraged me to think differently.

Following that approach, I created an acronym for SAFETY.

Safety: Seen, Acknowledged, Free, Enlightened. Trust Yourself.

SEEN:
Being seen by others and having the courage and fortitude to be seen, which means you will likely be vulnerable.

You don't hide nor live in fear about what others think of you. You show up as yourself and for yourself.

ACKNOWLEDGED:
Being surrounded by people who recognize and embrace you, your presence, and your contribution to their life.

To be acknowledged by others feels strong and powerful. This is not the same as seeking validation. It is about truly connecting to someone and their intentions and embracing their existence.

FREE:
Living by your own design. Not getting caught up in others' expectations of you, your values, and your lifestyle.

ENLIGHTENED:
Being expansive and open in your mindset. Recognizing there can be multiple outcomes to a situation. Employing a sense of curiosity in your approach to life. Surrendering to a higher power when you know you've done all you can.

TRUST YOURSELF:
Being vulnerable when necessary. Having faith. Knowing when to persist versus when to surrender. Trusting yourself is at the core of being safe. When I learned to trust myself, my instincts, my intuition, and the guidance by which I am surrounded, beautiful opportunities unfolded and continue to appear.

Sometimes we can't see beyond what we know, what we believe, or what we've experienced. Oftentimes we can't see the possibilities. We need to trust, especially ourselves.

So many unknowns remain for me, with my biological family, with my adoptive family, with my work, and with my career. Despite not knowing the outcomes, I feel safe and can handle anything that comes my way. I know I can create new opportunities, friendships, support systems, connections, programs, and careers.

If I decide something is worth pursuing, I do it.

Knowing how to ground myself and find safety on my own is the last big breakthrough for now.

That does not mean I never feel threatened or unsafe, but those times are not as prevalent. They do not take over my days the way they have in the past. I no longer live in survival mode. I don't feel the need to hide. I own my truth and allow my heart's desires to direct my actions.

This journey from limiting beliefs of abandonment to understanding my biological roots has come full circle into an understanding that no matter what happens, I will be okay. If I can trust myself, I can be seen, acknowledged, free, and enlightened. My growth is ongoing, and my evolution continues.

I celebrate all I've done and experienced. The good and the bad count equally because the lessons have helped me become who I am.

I remain excited for all that is to come.

Thank you for being on this journey with me. I hope that no matter where you are in your own, you pause and celebrate yourself. This is the time to get real with what you know and what you believe. Find that story you've been telling yourself and see if you can identify new data to support a different version.

Having the experience to rewrite my story, thanks to Deanna Moffitt, was a huge gift to me and started the next phase of my healing. I was open to where the work took me and have no regrets about how that has played out. I don't think the work ever truly ends, but it feels less like work and more like a practice and an integration of skills.

I invite you to get clear about what safety means to you and chart your course. I encourage you to trust yourself. Whether this is a beginning for you, or you are already on your own growth journey, know you are not alone.

ACKNOWLEDGMENTS

The support I have received in writing this book has been overwhelming. Having these incredible people as part of my author community has been such a blessing. Thank you for your belief in me and your support.

Adan Ruiz
Alana Madrid
Alex Cortez
Alexis Espinoza-Arrubla
Alicia and Dave Smith
Amanda Meyncke
Amanda Murdolo
Amiee and Henry Kolenovsky
Ana King
Anderson Hidalgo
Angelic Merrill
Anita Campana
Anita Medellin Hohnecker
Ann O'Hara
Ann Setter
Anne-Marie Shelley
Anthony Santoro
Ariana Madera
Arlene Dunbar-Pillsworth
Barbara DeMaio
Barbara Gouze
Barbie Giusto
Barrett Leigh
Berqui Rodriguez
Betsy Echevarria
Bob Guilbert
Brenda Burlbaugh
Brian Cohen
Brian Roces
Bryan Smith

Carol and Bob Miller
Carolin and Gerard
   Brickman
Caroline Christie
Cathy and Joe Ingrassia
Cheryl Thompson
Chris and Kim Austin
Christina Amador
Christopher Haretos
Claire Freire
Colleen Anderson
Constantinos Saittis
Cristina and Mike Alcaide
Damien and Annie Matias
Dana and Rebecca Paar
Daneene Christmas
Dave Cava
Deanna Moffitt
Deepak Thadani
Denise Focarino
Denise, Rafael, and Danielle
   Arboleda
Donna Downing
Eden and Chuck Cook
Eileen Logan
Elizabeth and Joselito
   Hidalgo
Elle Ruth
Emily Baker
Eric Koester
Erin Shea Murray

Felicia Casullo-Walker
Francia Sandoval
Frank Cruz
Frank Retselas
Gabriela Ruiz
Gerald Busardo
Gina D'Elia-Garcia
Greg Lakis
Guy Baroan
Gwen Bass
Heather Kurkierewicz
Holly Niedzielski
Irene Caldwell
Jackie and Gabby Astacio
Jacqueline and Eric Mueller
Jemsy Jimenez
Jenna Chouinard
Jennifer Carberry
Jennifer Carter
Jennifer Duman
Jeremy Jimenez
Jim Goetz
Jim Iemma
Jim Raia
Jim Zurlo
Jody Davidson
John and Lorraine Azzinaro
Joshua and Jenna Lande
Judenys Hidalgo
Judith Hidalgo
Judith Singleton

Karin Morris
Kathy Bell
Katie Johnson
Kelly Nagel
Kelly Sander
Kim Stevens
Kristine Vo
Lara Riggio
Laura Portorreal
Lauren Purificato
Laurie Claeys
Lesleigh Watson
Leslie Chiorazzi
Leticia Negron
Linda, Rob, and Megan Paar
Liory Segura
Lisa Brock
Margaret Lowitzer
Maria Toddes
Maribel and Junior Ruiz
Maribel Nieves
Mark King
Marla Huhman
Martin Brophy
Maryanne Cartwright
Matthew Kosara
Maureen and Stewart Lande
Mei Zhang
Melanie DelValle
Melissa Soodeen
Michael DePalma

Michael Venti
Michael Wolf
Michael DePalma
Michelle Rey
Michele Yacovello
Natalia McQuilla
Nathalie Barrezueta
Nelson Gomes
Nicole and Frank Cammarano
Paul Kanick
Paula Dymond
Paula Shelley Rodgers
Philia Swam
Ramsy Jimenez
Raquel and Mike Colon
Robin Cohen
Roman Konotopskyj
Ron Cuevas
Ron Prentki
Rosemarie and Perry Egan
Samantha Schmitt
Shane Urbas
Shannon Saksaka
Shari Grant
Shari Smith
Sonia Barreno
Stacie Odrobina
Stacy Khreis
Susan O'Sullivan
Tamara Hall

Tawnya Healy
Taylor Scott
Teany Hidalgo
Tim Hornef
Timothy Thompson

Veronica Martin
Vincent Russo
Wendy Rosario
William Langan
Zachary Hidalgo

APPENDIX

INTRODUCTION

Johnston, Wm. Robert. 2022. "Historical International Adoption Statistics, United States and World." Johnston's Archive. November 12, 2022. https://www.johnstonsarchive.net/policy/adoptionstats.html.

Adoption Network. 2023. "US Adoption Statistics." Accessed April 10, 2023. https://adoptionnetwork.com/adoption-myths-facts/domestic-us-statistics.

CHAPTER 2

American Adoptions. 2023. "The Truth About Adopted Adults and Relationship Issues." Accessed January 18, 2023. https://www.americanadoptions.com/adoption/adopted-adults-relationships.

Roizen, Sara. 2009. "The Primal Wound." *Art Therapy Spot* (blog). August 26, 2009. https://arttherapyspot.com/2009/08/26/primal-wound/.

CHAPTER 3

Karanova, Pamela. 2014. "Every Story Has a Struggle—The Key Is Finding Purpose in the Pain." *Finding Purpose in the Pain—One Adoptee's Journey from Heartbreak to Hope and Healing* (blog). Accessed January 13, 2022. https://pamelakaranova.com/.

Winfrey, Oprah. 2010. "Mother Reunites with Her Daughter After 42 Years Of Searching for Her." The Oprah Winfrey Show. 2010. 8:26. https://www.youtube.com/watch?v=ztcU6eQab3I.

CHAPTER 6

Brown, Brené. 2010. "Power of Vulnerability." Filmed December 2010 at TEDX Houston, TX. Video, 20:03. https://www.ted.com/talks/brene_brown_the_power_of_vulnerability.

Restrepo, Sandra, director. 2019. *The Call to Courage*. Netflix. 76 minutes. https://www.netflix.com/title/81010166.

CHAPTER 9

Hadnes, Myriam. 2018. "Thanks for the Feedback! Why We Struggle to Receive Well and What We Can Do About It." *Myriam Hadnes* (blog), *LinkedIn*. January 17, 2018. https://www.linkedin.com/pulse/thanks-feedback-why-we-struggle-receive-well-what-can-myriam-hadnes/.

Brown, Brené. 2022. *The Gifts of Imperfection 10th Anniversary Edition*. New York: Random House.

Santamarina-Hidalgo. 2020. "Since its tbt I figured I would share a little more of my personal journey. If you happened to catch my video from Saturday I shared a little about my background. I was adopted but only found out when I was 25. When I was 3 my mother and her husband (my namesake Santamarina) divorced and I didn't have much of a relationship with him.

I mentioned he passed recently, and his daughter was kind enough to reach out to me to share that she found photos and a letter I wrote to him. That was in March of 1981, and I had just turned 14. A lot happened that year now that I recall. The package came last night. These are the photos and the letter. I learned some things last night about who knew about my history when I didn't even know. If my mom could tell me her version of this story she would say she was protecting me, and on some level I know she was. My mom is still alive but not sure I'm ready to broach any of this with her just yet. I can now choose how I handle this. These choices affected a lot of aspects of my life, especially when it comes to things like fear of abandonment or lack of self-esteem (why would anyone choose me?). I have grown a lot and continue to do work on myself. Most recently inner child work, around my 7 year old self. Ironically pink dress photo is 7 year old me!!! The layers of our lives are verses in our story or chapters in our book. I created this group primarily to find my voice in a safe place. As I consider what I want next for my life professionally and personally it means a lot that I can share my own story (in real time in this particular case). There is no expectation that any of you need to do the same but know that this group exists to create connection, positivity and support. Without even knowing it I lived the first 25 years of my life out of alignment with my most authentic self, I cannot afford to waste any more days living out others versions of who I am or expected to be. I want to own my truth and move forward with as much grace and compassion as I can. I'm human so I will falter, and some days I won't even want to face it. But today, I feel that this newly discovered data about my existence gives me strength and hope. We all have our own versions of disappointments, trauma, victories, people who have had strong influence on us.

How comfortable are you with your story? I know this is deep for a Thursday! Thank you for holding space for me. I remain in constant gratitude for all of you." Facebook (private group), October 15, 2020.

CHAPTER 10
Slaton, Pamela. 2012. *Reunited: An Investigative Genealogist Unlocks Some of Life's Greatest Family Mysteries.* New York: St. Martin's Griffin Publishing.

CHAPTER 12
Brown, Brené. 2012. "Listening to Shame." Filmed March 2012 at TEDX Houston, TX. TED video, 13:20. https://www.ted.com/talks/brene_brown_listening_to_shame.